FROM NIGHTLIFE TO *Eternal Life*

The Story of Bitt Thrower

JIM HENNINGER

WESTBOW PRESS®
A DIVISION OF THOMAS NELSON
& ZONDERVAN

Copyright © 2018 Jim Henninger.

All rights reserved. No part of this book may be used or reproduced by any means, graphic, electronic, or mechanical, including photocopying, recording, taping or by any information storage retrieval system without the written permission of the author except in the case of brief quotations embodied in critical articles and reviews.

This book is a work of non-fiction. Unless otherwise noted, the author and the publisher make no explicit guarantees as to the accuracy of the information contained in this book and in some cases, names of people and places have been altered to protect their privacy.

WestBow Press books may be ordered through booksellers or by contacting:

WestBow Press
A Division of Thomas Nelson & Zondervan
1663 Liberty Drive
Bloomington, IN 47403
www.westbowpress.com
1 (866) 928-1240

Because of the dynamic nature of the Internet, any web addresses or links contained in this book may have changed since publication and may no longer be valid. The views expressed in this work are solely those of the author and do not necessarily reflect the views of the publisher, and the publisher hereby disclaims any responsibility for them.

Any people depicted in stock imagery provided by Thinkstock are models,
and such images are being used for illustrative purposes only.
Certain stock imagery © Thinkstock.

ISBN: 978-1-9736-1447-0 (sc)
ISBN: 978-1-9736-1449-4 (hc)
ISBN: 978-1-9736-1448-7 (e)

Library of Congress Control Number: 2018900451

Print information available on the last page.

WestBow Press rev. date: 01/22/2018

PROLOGUE

In mid-2015, I was invited to lunch with the youth minister of First Baptist Church in Cumming, Georgia. I had known him for about fourteen years and taught high school Sunday school classes under his direction. He wanted me to meet a man who was interested in having a book written about his life, detailing his journey from running nightclubs and engaging in illegal activities to finally becoming a committed Christian. That's how I came to meet Bitt Thrower at a Cracker Barrel restaurant in Cumming.

I immediately liked him, and he christened me Mr. Jim. He spoke in a deep, rich, resonant voice and was physically imposing at well over six feet and 275 pounds. He put me at ease when talking of his love for Jesus, his family, and his church. He explained that he had health issues and wanted to have his life story put in writing in the event it might help someone who needed to turn his or her life over to Jesus. He went so far as to say that if one person read an account of his life and then made a positive spiritual decision, any and all efforts spent to make that happen would have been more than worth it.

So I began a journey with Bitt over the next fifteen months to chronicle his life. We met for two to three hours at a time, and I recorded his recollections. I have approximately fifty-five to sixty hours of his comments, all of which he shared in his home or by the pool in his backyard. In this book, he weaves a fascinating story of action, danger, love, courage, good decisions, poor decisions, and redemption.

Since this is Bitt's story, I did only minimal research in documenting his recollections. He impressed me as having a prodigious memory for events but not for specific dates, so there may be some inaccuracies with respect to the exact timing presented in these pages. Additionally, some individuals may be unintentionally misidentified or have their names misspelled. In fact, for most of the people mentioned in these pages, I made up fictitious names for legal reasons. There might be other errors in this book, but rest assured they are also unintentional and, hopefully, minor in nature. It is my firm belief that this biography is a true depiction of the events Bitt lived, witnessed, and experienced.

Bitt's health began to falter as we worked on this project into the late summer of 2016. We formed a bond of friendship during our discussions, and I was repeatedly amazed by the multitude of things he experienced in his life. Of note, I created a rough draft of a manuscript as we worked our way through his story, and he read it piece by piece during the times we met. Looking back, I am happy we followed this approach, as it allowed him to have input into the formation of the entire book with the exception of the prologue and epilogue. He was pleased with the results of our efforts, and I hope you will be too.

CHAPTER 1

Bitt Thrower, known on paper as Howard Phillip Thrower, was a successful man who reflected on his position in life in the fall of 2004 as he sat by the hot tub and pool at his Atlanta area estate. Surrounding him were the fruits of his efforts, including an eight-thousand-square-foot house with five bedrooms, five and a half bathrooms, a private lake, a barn and stables, an indoor swimming pool, an Escalade, a Jeep, two Corvettes, a Hummer, an outdoor basketball court, an impressive gun collection, and titles to three other upscale homes, along with plenty of liquor, cash, and other assets.

He thought back to when he was baptized as a ten-year-old in a Southern Baptist church, soon after which he discovered a major skill: the strength and ability to blast a baseball out of the park. Bitt was engaging in his normal Sunday night routine of relaxing in a hot bathtub, reading the Sunday *Atlanta Journal Constitution* newspaper, and drinking two fingers of Johnnie Walker Blue. His sons and twin one-year-old daughters were fast asleep in their upstairs bedrooms, so he settled in for a nice read before turning in himself.

Bitt stayed busy running two nightclubs, Peaches and Platinum 21, and an auction and warehousing business at the time. Peaches, where he was the manager, had become the number-two seller of champagne out of fifty Atlanta-area clubs. Bitt's official title was general manager of operations, and he worked with a man named Bob Ireland, who had brought him into the nightclub industry as well as other hustles and money-making ventures.

He attended a Baptist church in Newnan, near his forty-acre residence. After working all night Saturday at Peaches, he took his son, stepson, and twin girls to worship services that morning on no sleep. This was part of his usual routine. He was a believer but not a practitioner of faith. The nanny was off on Sundays, and the six-foot-three, 300-pound, gravelly voiced Bitt intended to wind down before going to bed. After a bubble bath, he took his drink and a cigar to his deck to read and relax. He had spent the day grilling steaks and watching the kids swim. He also had played baseball in the meadow with the boys while the girls played in the barn.

Addicted to money but not power, Bitt enjoyed his relationships with politicians, celebrities, and professional athletes. He felt these important people were, in a manner of speaking, at his beck and call. He talked on the phone with many of the famous, including Earvin "Magic" Johnson on a couple of occasions. He rubbed shoulders with various entertainers, such as Rod Stewart, many of whom liked to be around the beautiful dancers in the club scene. Bitt was just the man to make entertainment arrangements for his well-known customers and acquaintances.

Bitt could drink large amounts of alcohol but usually refrained from heavy consumption. After reading the sports section, he reflected for a brief time on an agreement, more like a plea, he had made to God recently. He wanted God to spare his boys from following in his footsteps. He had some blood-pressure issues, was overweight, and didn't exercise. A workaholic, he figured that every hour he slept cost him at least $160 in tips at one of the clubs. Hence, working all night on Saturdays was profitable. Despite his activities, he had a spark of good in him that kept peeking out. He donated food items and blow-up houses for kids at the local church. He was also a generous giver to the offering plate on Sunday mornings, although he always gave cash and never wrote checks or put his name on a donation envelope.

Relaxing on his deck, he thought briefly of his third wife, from whom he had been legally separated for several years. She was the mother of his girls and would die of breast cancer in the years to come. He finished the sports section of the paper and relaxed. He thought about all of the things he had purchased that were stored on his farm and filled his oversized garage and barn. Many of them were in unmarked boxes. There were building materials, poker machines, Masters Golf sportswear, designer clothes, machine guns, and all manner of items to the extent that he had no exact idea what he owned. He bought two to three cars at a time and routinely purchased various items by the truckload to later sell out of his warehouse or at local auctions.

Most of his acquisitions were made through contacts with customers at the clubs. He never ceased to be amazed at what women and whiskey would bring to the table for him in terms of deals for clothing and goods. He felt as if he were on top of the world with the wildly successful Platinum 21, which employed 120 dancers a night, and Peaches, which drew celebrities and the office, instead walking among the patrons, encouraging them to spend on drinks and female companionship. This approach boosted business and fostered popularity, not to mention money, for him. He concluded, dressed in a bathrobe from the swanky Las Vegas hotel Rio as he sat, that he was vastly successful and thought to himself, *I have arrived. Look at what I've done.*

Out of the blue, Bitt heard a noise that startled him. He jumped up and began looking around. He grabbed a .45 and put a compact .40 in his robe pocket. He knew there were people who had things against him, which was one reason he always kept guns close by, even though he never carried one. After racking up the .45, he checked the kids' bedrooms first. They were all seemingly asleep, although he wondered if his boys had snuck out of their room to prank him.

He returned to the deck and heard something again. This time, he could tell it was a voice, a distinctive one, but its words were unintelligible. Bitt turned on all of the outdoor security lights around the house, the outbuildings, and the pasture, but he saw nothing. He again thought about the chances of someone coming to harm him—a real possibility, given his past. He wondered why someone would come all the way out to his home, when it would have been easy to get to him at work or in one of his cars. All of a sudden, he heard a voice, clear and forceful, say, "How do you expect to go to heaven if you've never read my Book?"

Bitt was terrified. He tossed his whiskey in one direction and his cigar in another. He kept Bibles all over the house, and he grabbed one after hustling inside. He began reading it that night, but he did so as if it were just a book, not the Word of God. He didn't make it through Genesis that night and retained little, if anything, he read. But it was a start. It was his turning point, and although he struggled over the next eighteen months to read through it, he did, and he eventually called the Bible his "blueprint for life." There were plenty of detours taken on both sides of the law before and after he reached that point in his life. This book is that story.

CHAPTER 2

Howard Phillip Thrower was the fourth of five children, born on October 7, 1957. Bitt and his two brothers and two sisters were raised in a stable environment in the LaGrange, Georgia, area. There were a couple of brief stays in Atlanta and Pensacola when his father relocated for job opportunities. While in Pensacola for a short time, Bitt played Little League baseball with the eleven- and twelve-year-olds when he was only eight years old. That was when it became apparent to him that he was a gifted athlete. However, the majority of Bitt's childhood was spent in LaGrange, where his father owned and operated a full-service gas station. Bitt spent lazy summers washing cars at the gas station, shooting baskets, and working out in a local gym.

Bitt was indoctrinated into a love for sports by his father, an exceptional athlete who starred in collegiate track in the shot put, the discus throw, and the hundred-yard dash. He was also a three-sport star in football, basketball, and baseball in high school. He was an all-state selection in football and was interested in any sport involving a ball that bounced or rolled. Bitt's mother, who didn't finish high school, grew up in an era before there were opportunities for girls in sports. Despite this, she played sandlot ball with all of her kids, and as Bitt remembered, "She spent a lot of time with me and my siblings teaching us to pitch, catch a baseball, and punt a football."

All of the Thrower children went to the same elementary school, junior high school, and high school. Bitt followed in his brothers' footsteps and was an all-around high school athlete. He flirted briefly with playing football, but baseball was his forte, and he didn't want to risk an injury. He also played basketball and tossed the shot put in track for one season. Bitt was a grinder in basketball while playing center at only six foot three. He worked hard and gave 100 percent to make up for his lack of speed and skill on the court. One of his former hoops coaches remarked that Bitt played every game with a bent elbow—in other words, he was always ready to shoot. He began playing school basketball in the fifth grade after being trained by his older brother John in grueling one-on-one sessions that honed his skills. Despite being seriously undersized height-wise, Bitt's teams were big winners in his eighth-, ninth-, and tenth-grade seasons. Then, as a junior, he earned a starting spot in the middle of the season on a squad that reached the final four of the state playoffs.

Instead of continued success, Bitt experienced one of his few setbacks in sports—or in life, for that matter. A new coach was hired, and he benched the seniors in favor of talented sophomores long on potential but short on experience. The season ended early for Bitt and a few other seniors who were not getting significant floor time. They quit in the middle of a ten-win season after feeling confident and looking forward to a senior season in basketball with lots of promise. It was quite a step down from the previous year. An incident in the locker room led to Bitt leaving the team. One of the younger players, the beneficiary of generous playing time, stole something from Bitt's locker. A locker-room confrontation followed, and Bitt acted out his frustration with his fists. The sticky-fingered teammate was dismissed from the squad, but Bitt decided enough was enough, and he left voluntarily.

This was a blessing in disguise, as he began playing recreational basketball for the local Hi-Y and Key Club teams. He ended up playing for a squad that finished as runners-up in Georgia, and he was free to take lots of shots, pouring in as many as forty points in a few contests. He was named to the all-state team at that level and also participated in a church basketball league. Also, the decision to leave the school basketball team left him free to concentrate on his first love and his real strength: baseball. He was the number-one pitcher for Troup High School and also played first base as he presented a big target for the infielders. He honed his game before reaching high school by playing with a local American Legion team at the age of thirteen. He was four to five years younger than many of his teammates and opponents, some of whom were collegiate players at home for the summer.

Although Bitt was an accomplished baseball player both on the mound and in the batter's box, a rival school was the stronger baseball program in the county. Bitt was clearly a big fish in a little pond. However, some trouble loomed for him. A new baseball coach decided Bitt had an attitude, and Bitt played little in his junior year. He wasn't allowed to pitch in even one game, but he refused to quit. His stock with college baseball recruiters, as one would expect, dropped as a result of being benched. With a new coach, he pitched several complete games during his senior season and contributed more than his share of hits, but he had little to show for it in the win column.

Bitt was also seeing firsthand the implementation of integration in the school system, and it was a struggle for many of the students. Although he was only an average student, he excelled in befriending and playing with black student athletes, especially on the basketball squad. He found that he got along well with black teammates who respected his fire and competitive bent. He played sandlot basketball with the more accomplished black players at the local park. Bitt was no angel and went along with his friends on two occasions for some sexual experiences with some of the looser girls in the area. As a result, he and several other boys contracted and were treated for syphilis. Fortunately, his parents never found out, and all of the infected boys were treated by the county health department at the school.

He never had a car in school. He asked his dad for one and expected to be turned down. To his surprise, Mr. Thrower told him he could have one and took him to a local Chevrolet dealer. After deciding on which vehicle he wanted, he sat down with the salesman, who asked him how he was going to pay for it. Bitt realized his dad was teaching him a lesson, and he would have to wait and earn the money to buy his first car. This was to happen a few years later, when he bought a Grand Prix while working on his first job.

Bitt graduated from high school in 1975 and soon began working for Big Star Grocery Store. He landed a union job as a bagger, buggy pusher, and stocker. He stayed with Big Star for five years, eventually becoming the manager of the frozen food and dairy departments. At first, he played developmental baseball for the Canton Redlegs and had a good summer season with twenty-two home runs. A short time later, he began to play semipro softball for a local team that consisted of all black players except for him. This team was formed and coached by a well-known former local athlete who recognized that Bitt was a gifted athlete.

While playing in a softball tournament, Bitt learned of a tryout for the baseball team at Chattahoochee Valley Community College in Phenix City, Alabama. He had only played softball since graduating from high school but decided to see if he could still hit a baseball. He prided himself on being willing to "take a shot at any crazy thing" and went to Phenix City. In 1977, collegiate baseball had just begun to use aluminum bats instead of the wooden ones used by the professional leagues. Bitt would quickly find out that aluminum bats propelled a ball significantly farther than standard wooden ones. Bitt took his turns in the batter's box, and he shined. He was a couple of years older than most of the other kids trying out and used his maturity and impressive strength to his advantage.

Bitt hit seven of the first ten pitches he saw out of the park, quickly getting the attention of the coaching staff. After crushing balls off of three different pitchers, Bitt was immediately on the radar of the head coach. The staff was amazed and wondered where he'd come from and what he had been doing to be able to step in and launch rockets off of accomplished pitchers. He received a scholarship offer on the spot after manhandling several of the hurlers currently on the Chattahoochee squad.

Bitt participated in the fall workouts the next semester while continuing to commute sixty-five miles back and forth so as to keep his job at Big Star. He stayed enrolled at Chattahoochee and played the forty-game fall practice schedule, during which he scrimmaged against some major programs, including Ohio State, Wisconsin, and Michigan State. One Chattahoochee coach was high on Bitt, although Bitt wasn't a polished player in the field.

Despite the fact he wasn't technically skilled, he even got some looks at catcher.

He was in school for a year but didn't stay involved, and by the spring, he had left the team. He simply tired of commuting back and forth between Phenix City and LaGrange, but he never quit playing softball. He was dominant in campus workouts and drew the attention of the Chattahoochee basketball coach, who invited him to try out for the team. He found he didn't completely buy into the whole college scene, and he gave it up. He maintained his job at Big Star and was strongly recruited by a local powerhouse softball team, something that would become a routine occurrence. He also played in the local men's basketball league in LaGrange and was good for twenty to twenty-five points per game against many former college players.

Bitt was recruited by the Canton Redlegs and the Target Advertising softball squad, formerly known as the Troup County Merchants. He had been working at Big Star for about four years by the age of twenty-one. However, he first got his feet wet in the world of work by obtaining a work visa at age fourteen. He clocked in during the summer and on weekends at a cotton mill before going to another part-time job while in high school, this one at Signal Knitting Mill. The mill produced pocket T-shirts, and Bitt and a coworker would occasionally "liberate" several grosses of them. They enlisted the services of a few of the school district bus drivers to sell them right out of the boxes to students on the way to school in the mornings and on the way home in the afternoons. The shirts sold for a dollar apiece, and Bitt and his friend made fifty cents on each sale. The bus drivers loved the chance to make extra money, and they also pocketed fifty cents per sale. It soon seemed as if every kid at Troup High had a nice pocket T-shirt, and Bitt's take on this was $300 to $400 a month. This scheme lasted for about six months and was his first taste of "creative entrepreneurism."

During his senior year of high school, he landed an elite part-time job at a local business, Phillips 76 Truck Stop. He pumped gas and learned to hustle. He received a small commission of twenty-five cents for selling quarts of oil and also earned tips for washing big rigs. Local high school athletes were catered to by truck stop management, and Bitt and others were allowed to work after school, after practices, and on weekends. Becoming more confident and bold, he conjured up an ambitious heist scheme while in the employ of the truck stop.

Bitt and an older friend became familiar with the lot lizards at the local truck stop. These were the female prostitutes who entertained the drivers in the privacy of their cabs' living quarters while the trucks were parked. Bitt and his friend became acquainted with a high-end hooker who agreed to help them in a little scheme they had thought up. The call girl drugged an unsuspecting driver in a nearby hotel room, incapacitating him for hours. She did this for the promise of $500, which Bitt paid her with money he'd saved from working for his dad. While the driver was out, Bitt and a coworker stole his truck on Friday night and drove it all the way to the docks in Miami, Florida. His colleague knew where to take it, and they sold the contents of the truck within six hours. Of course, the transaction was conducted in cash.

The refrigerated truck had forty thousand pounds of boxed beef in it. With no black market selling experience, Bitt and his partner agreed to part with the contents of the truck for $20,000 cash. They left the truck parked in a dockside lot and, with $10,000 in each of their pockets, caught a homeward-bound bus for an all-night ride. They made it back for their next shift the following Monday night. No one was the wiser, it seemed, and Bitt had his first stash. He kept it under his mattress and used it sparingly here and there over the next several years when he needed some money. He limited himself to withdrawing $100 to $300 at a time and later moved the cash to a similar hiding place under his new bed when he moved to Atlanta.

Bitt was taken to church services on a regular basis by his mother until he was about fifteen years old. He stopped attending for the most part when he started working nights after school. He eventually quit working at the truck stop and started at Big Star Grocery just before graduating from Troup High School. His affiliation with the Target Advertising softball team kept him busy for the next four years or so as he and his teammates drove to high-level weekend tournaments for six months out of the year.

In 1978, Bitt learned of an open tryout for a professional slow-pitch softball team in the Atlanta area, under the sponsorship of Miller Beer. He and two teammates, Odie Collyer and Bruce Judger, went to the tryout. Collyer was well known in LaGrange as an outstanding basketball player, and Judger had recently been released from a National Football League team. Only Collyer and Judger were officially invited to attempt to make the team, which was considered a sure thing for them more than a tryout. Bitt, a quiet and shy guy at the time, wasn't formally invited and considered himself an afterthought in comparison to his two talented friends. He went to a Miller Beer Rangers tournament at the insistence of Collyer and Judger on only a few hours' sleep. They insisted Bitt take his playing gear with him in the event he might get the chance to show his stuff. He did so, believing he probably wouldn't be asked to play while his two buddies solidified their roles on their new team.

Bitt was exposed to massive players who were bulked up to the point that he suspected many of them were on steroids. The team's manager had invited a number of players to show up and was mixing and matching them in different lineups during a tournament against high-quality competition. Bitt watched one giant of a man hit four pop-outs as he swung just under the ball to go hitless in the first game. As luck would have it, several of the gassed-up players left after the first game, and Miller was shorthanded for the next contest. The coach asked Collyer and Judger if the big guy watching was available to play. Bitt played in the next two games and cracked seven home runs in nine at bats, making the most of his opportunity. Even though the coach called him Big Charlie for some reason, Bitt was invited to come back and play on Sunday. He told the coach he was scheduled to work at Big Star tomorrow and didn't want to forego the eight dollars an hour if he wasn't needed. He was assured he would play.

Showing up the next day with Collyer and Judger, Bitt quickly noticed there were several more players present to play for the Rangers who hadn't been there for the second and third games twenty-four hours earlier. Bitt, relegated to the bench, was angry, and he threw a few bats around before leaving the dugout and watching from the stands. Miller won the tournament handily, and Bitt and his two friends returned to LaGrange. He forgot about the Rangers. Collyer and Judger were heavily recruited to play by Miller, who enticed them with the trappings of a professional softball team. They looked forward to flying to tournaments, receiving meal money, and being paid a weekly stipend. Miller representatives mailed cards to Collyer and Judger with tickets to Atlanta Braves games and some hundred-dollar bills. Judger, who owned and operated a successful LaGrange-area business, agreed to play on one condition: Bitt had to be added to the roster too.

Thus, Bitt made the fourteen-man roster for Miller Beer but was considered the last man on the bench. He was paid $300 a weekend and given meal money as well as the use of an apartment in the Atlanta area to be shared with another player. Bitt was a pro. The Rangers began practicing in January 1979. Miller Beer played weekend tournaments and was in the twenty-team Super Slow-Pitch Conference sanctioned by the ASA USSSA. During practice sessions, Bitt shined and earned the cleanup spot in the batting order by the beginning of the season. It was not unusual for guys to be brought in and looked at in game conditions to see if management wanted to add them to the roster. Scouts were utilized to identify possible players on other teams. This was Bitt's first taste of big-time softball, as characterized by the dozens of extravagant uniform combinations sported by the players. At least fifty players were evaluated during the season in attempts to improve the squad.

Bitt played about 110 games that first summer, and he hit more than ninety home runs. His move to Atlanta to play softball now seemed like a permanent one. Living in the Gold Key Apartments in Riverside, Georgia, Bitt landed a daytime job with State Farmer's Market in the meat department. The apartment complex sponsored a softball team, and Bitt played with them too. He met several up-and-coming people at the Gold Key complex, including Thurston Taylor of the NFL's Philadelphia Eagles. Bitt, along with many others, considered Taylor a great athlete, partially because he was gifted with 4.4 speed in the forty-meter dash.

CHAPTER 3

Bitt's horizons were widening from a social standpoint as a result of living in the upscale Gold Key apartment complex, which housed mostly singles. He and his roommate, Judger, were playing for pay for the Gold Key softball team and for other squads in Atlanta and LaGrange when they weren't tied up with Miller Beer. Judger slapped singles to set the table for Bitt and the other sluggers on the team. In midseason, Judger suddenly tired of setting the table for the team's power hitters and decided to become a home run hitter himself. To everyone's surprise, he was more than capable of doing so and nailed more than a hundred dingers, primarily in the second half of the summer. Before long, Bitt's relationships with the opposite sex would ramp up, primarily in the nightclub environment, but for now, his life was all about playing ball and working at the State Farmer's Market.

Besides being a close friend and softball colleague, Judger also encouraged Bitt to attend church in LaGrange in the off-season, when their weekends weren't tied up. A committed Christian, Judger helped nourish the spiritual seed planted in Bitt's childhood. Another factor in encouraging Bitt's church attendance was the church basketball team that he and Judger joined in the winter of 1979. They were able to stoke their competitive juices against other men's teams in the LaGrange area and faced many former high school and college standouts.

Bitt dated a few girls in high school and continued to sporadically take someone out beginning in the early '80s. His first main squeeze was a straitlaced girl named Joanie. He soon developed a roving eye but was too busy for any serious relationships. While working at the Farmer's Market and playing softball, he got his first taste of serious working out. He began bodybuilding with buddies at European Fitness in Forest Park, an area not far from downtown Atlanta. His workouts started out clean, but he followed the circle after about six months and began using testosterone to boost his strength.

The next season, 1980, was a successful one for Miller Beer, as they won Georgia's highest-level softball tournament and qualified for the World Tournament. However, the ongoing costs during the season had taken a toll on Miller's purse strings. First-class seats on flights, elaborate uniforms, hotel accommodations, meal per diems, and players' salaries prompted the Miller organizer to inform the team that the money had dried up. Faced with the prospect of traveling to California by bus, the team refused to accept such mundane travel arrangements. As a result, the team immediately disbanded following a postgame meeting at the ball park and never reformed. Bitt was shocked and in a state of disbelief.

However, he was soon picked up by the LaGrange team he had previously left to play for Miller Beer. After Bitt received a phone call from one of his friends and former teammates, three players and two wives arrived at Bitt's Atlanta-area apartment at six o'clock in the evening. Against his better judgment, he jumped into his friend's borrowed Cadillac for a fourteen-hour drive to Peavey, Missouri, to play a 10:00 a.m. game. The team was loaded with talent from Georgia and Alabama, but their low energy, depleted from the all-night drive, led to a 26–5 defeat.

After a few hours of sleep, the team was raring to go by early afternoon. Bitt's squad was one of more than a hundred teams in the tournament. The LaGrange group and Red Man Tobacco from California turned out to be the top two entrants. All of the fans flocked to the LaGrange team's games to see home runs galore. They won eight games on the remainder of Saturday and eight more on Sunday. They were one of the final four teams on Monday but lost on a controversial call at two o'clock in the morning. That was the end of softball for Bitt in 1980.

Next year, he and Judger played for Mann's Veneer, a team organized by Jerry Link and sponsored by a nephew of Link. In the not-too-distant future, Link would hold the dubious distinction of being the first Georgian incarcerated for a RICO (racketeer influenced and corrupt organizations) conviction. Bitt started the summer on the bench for Mann's but replaced a player who was injured. He had a batting average of over .600 and hit seventy-five to eighty homers, but the squad was so deep that he didn't always hold down a starting position. He also played for Gold Key in 1981 and made $250 to $300 a week from each team, plus meal money.

He was still working during the week at the Farmer's Market and playing for pay on the weekends. The Mann's organizer, Link, was active in massage parlors, nightclubs, gambling interests, and prostitution rings. He also introduced Bitt into the world of organized crime. During a softball tournament in Columbia, South Carolina, the Saturday night game was rained out. However, Link asked Bitt to accompany him to the ballpark. Bitt was confused because the game was cancelled.

When they arrived, another car pulled up and parked nearby. Link gave Bitt a briefcase and asked him to take it to the other car and exchange it for a briefcase the occupant would be holding. Bitt did as he was told. The window of the other car rolled down, and two Hispanics were sitting in it. Bitt noticed a pistol on the seat in their vehicle. Alarmed, he hit the man in the passenger side with his briefcase, reached into the car, and took the gun. He held the gun on the two men and took their briefcase. Holding both briefcases, he then backed his way to the car Link was driving and took a seat. He'd decided he was going to take charge of the situation when he saw the gun. Link was taken aback and told Bitt, "We don't do things that way." Link jumped out of the car and walked over to apologize to the man Bitt had hit, who was suffering from a busted nose and lip.

Link turned over the briefcase Bitt was supposed to deliver to the men, along with their gun. He then returned to his car. He told Bitt that the men were his friends. Bitt replied that he should have told him more about what to expect. He added that the gun had scared him, so he'd taken it. Bitt learned that the Hispanics were buying five pounds of cocaine, and he received $1,000 for his participation, even though he'd nearly aborted the deal. He briefly considered taking back the cocaine from the Hispanics and also keeping their cash but decided he wouldn't know how to move the drugs. That was Bitt's first brush with illegal activity since the truck hijacking and the T-shirt scheme while in high school.

As a result of the cocaine exchange, he discovered something about himself: he enjoyed the action. It was exciting and gave him a rush. He'd made $1,000 for a few minutes of effort and was feeling his oats. He was still working for eight dollars an hour in the meat market, and he added his newly acquired funds to his mattress stash. Before long, Bitt would trade in his truck for a Ford LTD II. He was moving up in the world.

One of the coaches for Miller, Mac Honda, had taken Bitt to some parties that summer thrown by Link, introducing him to girls and champagne. He was beginning to see how the other half lived, specifically those on the other side of, or at least skirting, the law. He didn't know how to act at those parties, which were attended primarily by people in the sex, drugs, and prostitution industries. He felt out of place and intimidated despite his imposing size.

Never one to balk at some easy money, Bitt hooked up with a friend who had drug-running connections in Fort Lauderdale, Florida, in the late '70s. Almost as an afterthought, he accompanied his buddy to the Sunshine State a few times, and they piloted a bass boat to the Bahamas and back to pick up shipments. Each trip netted Bitt and his partner $5,000 in cash apiece for a five-hour round trip. This money went into his mattress stash along with his heist cash and his savings from Big Star. Bitt didn't know whom he and his friend were running the pot for, and he didn't want to know. He did realize the boats were stolen when he and his friend were told they could keep the boats if they desired. They decided it was the wisest course of action to leave the boats at the dock, and they did just that and hustled back to Georgia. He would return to Florida years later and get more heavily involved in moving drugs from the Caribbean into the States.

CHAPTER 4

Bitt quit working for Market Grocery in the State Farmer's Market in 1982 but not before he grew close to the owners. They invited him out to their ranch for cookouts. This represented another of the first times he got a taste of the good life. He was impressed that the owners owned a herd of buffalo and lots of other nice amenities. He left the grocer because new management came on board. His established work schedule called for him to work on Saturdays in the winter in return for not being required to work on Fridays in the summer. This allowed him to travel and play in weekend softball tournaments. His new supervisor revoked the arrangement for Fridays off in the summer and even threatened to require him to work on Saturdays, so Bitt turned in his notice after four years. His resignation ended his privilege of occasionally confiscating a box of steaks or other cuts of beef.

Bitt was proud that none of his softball teammates went hungry when he worked for Market Grocery, but it was time to move on.

Always coveted by strong softball teams, Bitt had just started playing the first of his two seasons for the Bee Hive, a liquor store sponsoring a class-A team in Atlanta. This squad was not at the elite level of his three previous teams, but they won the Georgia class-A state title. Bitt was the most talented player by a long shot and enjoyed his big-gun status. Even though the level of play was a step down, he still made $200 to $300 a week to play.

The Bee Hive was coached by Scott Behling, who learned that Bitt was out of work. Behling owned a painting company and hired him. Working for a boss who managed his softball team had its advantages, and Bitt was often paid even when he didn't show up for work. By this time, he was enjoying his active life. He loved playing ball for pay as well as occasionally showing up for work and receiving a full-time paycheck. Bitt began hanging out in his free time with Thurston Taylor, the tall and handsome former NFL tight end. Taylor showed Bitt how to dress and how to talk, basically grooming him to present himself as successful. Taylor was a chick magnet and always had a beautiful girl on his arm.

Bitt had a big season for the Bee Hive. He was still being picked up by other teams for games here and there, often earning fifty dollars to show up for one contest. He hit about 150 home runs that summer for the Bee Hive and was making a name for himself in softball circles. His friend Judger had moved on to another team, and Bitt shined brightly with a talented, although not elite, group of teammates. Behling told him he'd never coached a player who hit more than a hundred homers and was thrilled with his performance. The owner of the Bee Hive, Tim Zapf, also owned other businesses, including some biscuit establishments. Zapf was arrogant and sat in his lawn chair on the top of the dugout à la George Steinbrenner so he could yell encouragement or insults to his players.

A colorful gentleman and entrepreneur, Zapf built a nightclub, Stagger Lee's, on Old National Highway in South Atlanta. It was the only club on the south side of town with a dance floor, which was destined to make it wildly popular. Bitt was part of a crew put together by Behling to paint the club during its construction. He quickly took a liking to Zapf because he was generous. Zapf paid Bitt and the other workers in cash and only made them work half days on Fridays, although he paid them for the whole day. Additionally, he frequently had food catered to the job sites to feed the painters and other workers. Before long, Bitt noticed that some of the workers and subcontractors were stealing from Zapf. Supplies, such as lumber and other building materials, were disappearing on a regular basis. Not unfamiliar with the idea of taking something from an employer, Bitt was mad nonetheless. He reasoned that Zapf was treating everyone well and didn't deserve to have his building materials stolen.

Bitt went to some of the culprits and asked them if they had ever been treated so well by an employer. He reminded them that they were highly paid and frequently provided with food and drinks on the job. He then demanded that the stolen materials be returned from their personal pickup trucks, or they were going to experience "a real problem." A return of pilfered materials happened on two occasions following Bitt's persuasive suggestions. The threat of being manhandled by Bitt started a new trend and certainly reduced the expense burden for the construction project. His ability to physically intimidate others would serve him well in his future occupation.

Zapf got wind of the situation. He appreciated the fact that Bitt was looking out for his best interests and was willing to stand up for him. Near the end of the building project, he asked Bitt if he enjoyed painting, and Bitt stifled a laugh while admitting he really didn't. Zapf then inquired if he knew anything about nightclubs. Bitt answered honestly and replied that he didn't and had only been in one or two as a customer. Zapf then asked him to stay on with him and help him with his new club, Stagger Lee's. Bitt asked what he would do, since he considered himself to be country and not slick enough to work in a nightclub. Zapf told him he wanted him to be his head of security. Bitt was in the club on the day it opened and was proud of the high-quality silk T-shirt Zapf provided him. Bitt began earning $400 to $500 a week, and his career in nightclubs was under way.

CHAPTER 5

Bitt received a small weekly check from Zapf, as most of his earnings were made in cash. Soon the customers were coming in droves, lining up at the door to gain admittance. This was also the beginning of a reduction in the time Bitt could devote to playing softball, because he had to work Friday nights and Saturday nights from eight o'clock till dawn. As a result, he played more local ball, often on Saturday mornings and afternoons. He frequently played games on weekends with little or no sleep. However, his ability to travel to out-of-town tournaments went by the wayside. Bitt learned all about hustle over the next three to four years at Stagger Lee's. At first, he had no idea what people were doing in the line to enter the club when they held up their hand with money in it. Initially, Bitt just ignored them. Finally, someone Bitt later learned was a local drug dealer told him the idea was for him to walk the hand raiser immediately into the club in exchange for the cash, often a fifty-dollar bill, cupped in his palm. Bitt, with a sense of honesty and honor that never deserted him, informed the first gentleman he accommodated that he was still going to pay the cover charge and not stiff the club.

A few of the local College Park police force worked security in the parking lot at Stagger Lee's in plain clothes. They maintained order and enjoyed the club scene, although they stayed outside most of the time. Bitt found that one of the local moonlighting policemen, Terry Honda, loved the violence. He also developed a great affection for Bitt and became a loyal friend to him. Mr. Zapf was a hardworking and intelligent man but a little rough around the edges. He understood that the patrons had to feel a sense of security at the club and in its parking lot. The club employed a deejay, a showboat by the name of Gomer. He was an ex-marine and wore a tuxedo while spinning the hits. Shortly after the club opened, Gomer found out that Bitt had received a raise in his weekly salary. He also knew that Bitt pulled in a lot of tips and was driving Zapf's old car after the boss bought a new one. Actually, Bitt had purchased the car from Zapf at a fair price. Gomer told some of the policemen who worked security part-time that he wanted to kick Bitt's butt. One of them, Lieutenant Butler, told Gomer that his job was to spin records, while Bitt's was to break up fights and the like. Butler added that he should consider the fact that Bitt was adept at deflecting punches and delivering thunderous blows. Gomer thought better of his idea to confront Bitt.

In a short time, live bands became the norm, and the first group to play at Stagger Lee's did so because they were in the area when their previously scheduled engagement was cancelled. They called the club, and Bitt answered the phone. The group's manager said they were close by and would play that night for $200. They were the Cornelius Brothers and Sister Rose, and to Gomer's chagrin, they were a big hit. Their forte was their mastery of 1960s classic music hits, such as "Treat Her like a Lady." Cornelius made a big entrance with his gaudy clothes and stacked shoes. Their first show was a crowd-pleaser, and in the wee hours of the morning, when the doors were being locked, Zapf told Bitt to meet him in the morning so they could build a stage for future live acts. Bitt gave Zapf credit for instilling a great work ethic in him. Zapf's partner in the club, Alan Fields, made his daytime living in the dry-cleaning business, but Zapf ran the club almost single-handedly with Bitt's help. There were no exotic dancers at Stagger Lee's, as it was intended to be a dance club for patrons who paid the three-dollar cover charge and purchased high-priced drinks with bar food. The size of the club and its large dance floor were keys to its success. It was never a girlie club like the ones Bitt would become involved in later.

Early in the tenure of Stagger Lee's, Bitt and Zapf went for breakfast after visiting another club across the county line that could stay open until 4:00 a.m., as opposed to the 2:00 closing time Stagger had to observe. At about five o'clock in the morning, they returned to Stagger Lee's because Zapf had forgotten something. Soon after arriving, Zapf determined that the alarm system for the club had been disarmed. He and Bitt quietly entered the kitchen and found the club manager loading cases of liquor into the trunk of his car. The club had just observed a special night called Free Pour, an event soon after opening night designed to bring in lots of business. Therefore, the inventory of liquor would be guesswork after that particular evening. Zapf looked at the manager and then at Bitt. He told Bitt and the pilfering manager to put all of the cases back into the club. He then instructed Bitt to put the nervous manager in the trunk of his own car. Bitt complied but was worried that Zapf might have something gruesome in mind, including the disappearance of the thief. He then ordered Bitt to close the trunk. Bitt feared they were going to drive to a secluded area and dispose of the manager in some fashion. However, Bitt and Zapf simply left the manager in the trunk of his car and departed.

Bitt, who was relieved, went home and fell asleep. A few hours later, Bitt woke up to the sound of someone beating on his front door. It was Zapf, who told Bitt to get dressed and come with him. Bitt was worried again and thought it might have been smarter to do whatever Zapf had in mind while it was still dark a few hours ago. Zapf was in no hurry to go back to the club. He stopped by the bank and then gassed up his car. Zapf then pulled up to the car and opened the trunk. The would-be booze stealer was sweating profusely, as the temperature has risen dramatically in the closed quarters. Zapf looked at him and asked, "Are you going to be loyal to me now, or are you going to try to steal from me again?" The scared manager answered that he would never try to steal even a dime in the future and wouldn't allow anyone else in the club to do so either. Zapf smiled and pointed to Bitt, saying, "Bitt's going to keep an eye on you. If he thinks you're taking something—anything, really—he has my permission to take you out."

Bitt thought to himself, *Great. Now I'm the hit man.* From that point forward, Bitt unofficially ran the club. Understandably, the manager had no lost love for Bitt, but he caused no further trouble for him or Zapf.

Over time, Bitt began to dress more stylishly as he evolved into the role of a seater and greeter for the club's patrons. He picked up a lot of hustle money, which consisted of tips for cutting in line, preferred seating arrangements, and, eventually, female companionship. Bitt quickly learned that he had some authority at Stagger Lee's when people would treat him like an old friend for the favors and attention he provided to them. Pretty girls would show him their attention and drape themselves over his arms to his surprise and delight. He was getting a taste of the fast life, and he liked it. Bitt began to see opportunities to make a lot of money and improve his lifestyle. Many customers asked him why he didn't sell drugs to the patrons, because that could net him as much as $500 a night in tax-free cash. But Bitt was not interested in dealing drugs and refused the offers.

Bitt's sophistication in security methods and management

grew as he experienced being in the life. He became adept at taking cash offers to circumvent long lines at the entrance. He would announce that a customer in line, coincidentally flush with cash, had an emergency call and needed to follow Bitt into the club immediately. Eventually, he became arrogant and didn't bother with a front story. If another person in line complained, Bitt would tell him to shut up, or he would physically move him to the back of the line. His size and menacing demeanor served him well in these situations. He eventually changed from a humble guy happy to be playing ball who didn't need a whole lot to someone driven to make a lot of money and get the good things in life, such as luxury cars and big houses. For the most part, he quit playing softball, even on the local level, after a couple of years at Stagger Lee's. He lost his drive to compete in major softball leagues, although he was in the prime of his playing career.

Bitt met his first wife in the club, which became one of the biggest hot spots in Atlanta. The north side of town was ruled by the Limelight Club, while Stagger Lee's held domain on the south side. All other competing establishments were more pubs than clubs. Stagger Lee's, with live music and dancing, was the place to be seen in South Atlanta. Bitt continued to refrain from dealing in drugs at that time, although he had opportunities and offers to get seriously involved in it. He finally began dabbling in the drug trade by arranging for cocaine to be made available to the patrons of Stagger Lee's. He was educated in the art of diluting pure product after consistent customers were established. Soon the cocaine trafficking in the club went from an ounce or so a night to a kilo of product on a nightly basis only a month or two later. He avoided direct involvement and always used employees as intermediaries. This enterprise boosted his hustle money considerably. He also learned he had thunder in his hands at Stagger Lee's in his role as an enforcer and bouncer. He became adept at knocking out belligerent customers with his fists or choking them out with his strong hands by squeezing them in the larynx and inducing a temporary nap within a few seconds. He earned the nickname Dr. Spock for his ability to make troublemakers pass out.

Bitt first noticed the lady who was to become his first wife, Cindy Davenport, at Stagger Lee's on the arm of a flamboyant local attorney who was her fiancé for a short time. She was blonde and beautiful and swept Bitt off his feet. She had been married once before. She made it clear to Bitt that she wanted to spend time with him, even though she was currently engaged to the attorney.

Cindy was more advanced than Bitt in matters of intimacy and was raising a young daughter, Melissa.

Cindy came to the club on a Sunday, which was always a slow night, and left with Bitt to his apartment, where she stayed, marking the beginning of Bitt's first significant romance. She picked up her things from the palatial residence of her attorney boyfriend a short time later. She encouraged Bitt to be aggressive and make more money. Within a few months, Bitt bought a small but nice house in Jonesboro, Georgia, for his soon-to-be wife, and she began pushing him to do whatever it took to become wealthy and acquire nice things. Proving that there was still a little bit of boy in the man, Bitt took her on a honeymoon to watch him play in a weekend softball tournament. It was one of his last times on a softball field for several years.

Bitt kept Cindy stylishly attired in jewelry and nice clothes. He also gave her nice cars, but it wasn't enough. During one argument, Bitt used his elbow to smash out the window of Cindy's Mercedes-Benz. He repaired the window but not the relationship. They separated after about four years, following the birth of Bitt's first daughter, Bella. They divorced not long afterward. Bitt hadn't spent a lot of time at home while married to Cindy. He purchased a condo for her when they separated, but she moved out of it a year later to pursue a wealthy local businessman. For Cindy, life with Bitt had been nothing short of a roller coaster.

Despite a less-than-optimal home life during his marriage to her mother, Bitt made a huge impression on his stepdaughter Melissa, who loved him and considered him to be her real father. She met him when she was five years old and spent time around him for about eight years. He took her to an occasional softball game and to a bakery for doughnuts on Saturday mornings. Melissa accumulated a large collection of baseball cards and lots of designer clothes courtesy of Bitt. Living in the Jonesboro and Riverdale, Georgia, area at the time, she felt close to her stepfather and was comfortable talking with him about anything. She had a better relationship with him than she did with her mother, Cindy. Bitt even arranged for Melissa and her friends to go to some concerts in a limousine, which was pretty heady stuff for teenage girls. When Bitt and Cindy split, Melissa blamed her mother for the breakup and moved in with her grandparents. The time Bitt spent with her was special to Melissa, especially since she didn't have a relationship with her birth father.

CHAPTER 6

Bitt stayed at Stagger Lee's for four more years. He was involved in many altercations in the parking lot, where injuries and even homicides took place. He and his security staff tried to keep troublemakers out of the club. There were several shootings, and the big metal entrance door stopped bullets more than once. On one occasion, Bitt threw out a rowdy customer who, a short time later, unloaded a clip of nine shots at him while he was leaning against the front door. The bullet pattern resembled an outline of his body, but he wasn't hit. The shooter, never identified, left quickly and, to Bitt's knowledge, never returned to Stagger Lee's.

Shootings became more frequent at the club during its five-year run as men began using guns instead of settling disputes with their fists. There were four people killed in the club's parking lot, and one of them was a close friend, David Bledsoe. He was a huge man and had played football for Nebraska and the Denver Broncos. Bitt and Bledsoe originally met through the local softball leagues. He coached softball teams and was ten years Bitt's senior. He had a wife and two kids and worked a full-time job as a guard at a federal penitentiary. Bitt and Bledsoe worked as a team at the club, although Bitt was officially his boss. The security employees grew in number as the club grew in popularity, but Bitt took a special liking to Bledsoe, who treated Bitt like his little brother. The bouncers at the club were amazed at how rapidly Bledsoe could throw devastating punches that immediately incapacitated rowdy customers. However, he could turn his tough-guy persona off and on like a light switch. He was happily married, a good father, and a funny guy who reminded Bitt of the actor John Candy.

Shortly before Stagger Lee's closed its doors, Bitt kicked out two individuals trying to enter the club in improper dress. Both were dirty and looked as if they had come directly from a construction worksite. They were wearing T-shirts and didn't fit Stagger Lee's strict criteria for appearance. Bitt pointed to the dress-code rules posted on the wall near the entrance and informed them they would have to leave but were welcome to return if they cleaned up and changed into nicer clothes. Bledsoe came into the club and witnessed the two would-be customers arguing with Bitt. The taller of the two, frustrated by being denied admission, snapped off a quick punch right between Bledsoe's eyes. Not only was he not phased, but Bledsoe walked closer to the assailant and took a second shot before looking him in the eyes and saying, "Is that all you got? You're gonna pay now."

The altercation moved to the parking, where Bledsoe, at six foot six and 350 pounds, began bobbing and weaving with the aggressor, who landed no more punches. All the while, Bledsoe didn't throw one punch in retaliation. The conflict kept moving and worked its way across the street to the Target Center parking lot. The entire time, Bledsoe was dodging shots thrown at him and repeatedly telling his opponent, "I'm getting ready to hit you." All of a sudden, Bledsoe faked a right hook and landed a solid left to the jaw of the troublemaker, who went down in a heap like a sack of potatoes. Still angry, Bledsoe asked Bitt, who was watching, to hold the fallen fighter up. Bitt did so, and Bledsoe kicked him once in the face, sending him down again. Bitt kept him pinned to the ground.

The beaten man's friend, who witnessed the whole thing from

start to finish, including the kick to his buddy's face, pulled a gun out of his waistband. It was a long-barreled .357, and he shot Bledsoe once in the back. Bledsoe went down. To Bitt's surprise, the shooter didn't fire at him. Instead, he helped his friend, whom Bitt had released, get up, and they took off. Initially, Bitt thought Bledsoe was going to be okay. The bullet entry in his back looked small. However, when he turned Bledsoe over, he was shocked at what he saw. Bledsoe was obviously wounded in his abdomen. Bitt ran to the club and told a coworker to call an ambulance. He then ran back to Bledsoe and held him in his arms until the paramedics arrived. Bledsoe lost a lot of blood and was unresponsive. He was declared dead on arrival at the hospital.

Mrs. Bledsoe arrived at the hospital with her two small children and faced the awful truth that her husband was gone. Bitt checked on the widow and her children several times over the next few months to make sure they were getting along as well as possible. The shooter and his friend took off and were on the run from the local police. There were wanted posters and BOLO (be on the lookout) bulletins issued, and they were caught a week later following an anonymous tip. They had been hiding out in an apartment complex in the Atlanta area. One had shaved his head, and the other had dyed his hair another color. They'd also painted the truck they were using a new color. Both were in their early to midtwenties. After being picked up, they spent the night in jail and were released on their own recognizance the next morning despite being charged with murder. Bitt and other friends of Bledsoe's were not happy.

Within two weeks of the arraignment of the two accused, they were dead. One seemingly hung himself with his own belt and left a suicide note. The other appeared to have overdosed on twenty-four quaaludes and left an apology note for taking a husband and father away from his wife and two children. Both deaths were ruled to be suicides, and they occurred within a three-hour time period. Bitt was questioned several times by the police, but he had a strong alibi. Only a few people knew of a middle-of-the-night phone call made to Bitt at home a short time after the two accused murderers were released. A male voice who didn't identify himself informed Bitt that he and his family were going to be killed, and "the job would be finished." Bitt and his family left within thirty minutes of the call and checked into a motel room for a few days.

Bitt and an ex-military friend who worked at another local club tried to find the two suspects a few days after their release. They wore duster jackets with weapons concealed in the inside pockets and went to a few bars that were reportedly hangouts of the perpetrators to no avail. The suicide and overdose occurred within a week of the threatening call. A fact that didn't come to light until later was that the local police had identified and located two other individuals who had witnessed the parking lot shooting. As it turned out, their testimony wasn't needed. The police suspected Bitt knew more about the untimely deaths of the suspects than he was willing to share. He stayed true to his lifelong self-imposed rule of responding to questions from law enforcement: "'I don't know' ain't ever hurt anybody."

Before Bledsoe's shooting, Bitt confronted two members of the Outlaws motorcycle club who came into Stagger Lee's on a Sunday night and refused to take off their colors in violation of the dress code put in place by the owners, Zapf and Fields. The Outlaws' headquarters was located nearby, making an incident at some point in time inevitable. It was a slow Sunday night, and Bitt showed the two solo bikers that they weren't quite the men they thought they were. In his terms, he "hammered" the pair after they refused to remove the colors. After Bitt put them on the floor of the L-shaped entryway to the club, one of the bikers bolted out the door. With just one left in front of him, Bitt administered an "old-fashioned country lesson," which included some well-placed kicks to his midsection and head. Bitt knew that would not go over well with the club and its leadership, who were located less than a mile away. About ten minutes later, Bitt got to meet the entire club.

The Atlanta Outlaws roared into Stagger Lee's parking lot, and Bitt walked outside, thinking he might see five or six members. He was prepared to fight. But there were more than thirty of them. He knew he was in trouble and decided not to retrieve his equalizer, a softball bat in his truck. One biker stepped off of his machine. Bitt soon learned he was Chain, the club president. Bitt took Chain for a stone-cold killer after looking him directly in the eyes. Chain asked Bitt if he had hurt two of his guys, and Bitt admitted that he had. He patiently explained that they'd refused to remove their colors (their jackets). Chain said he and his guys wouldn't do that for anybody. He wanted to know what Bitt was going to do now that he was facing the entire club. Bitt responded that he was prepared to fight to the death if he had no other choice. Chain smiled and told Bitt, "I like you, big guy. Tell you what we're going to do." He then outlined a settlement of sorts: none of the Outlaws except Chain would ever set foot in the club. Chain and his old lady would come in when they wanted to and would sit at the end of the bar or in a corner. He would wear his colors but not flash them in front of customers' noses. Most importantly, all of the drinks he and his wife ordered would be free. Bitt replied that it sounded like a good enough deal, and they shook on it in the parking lot. Chain and his wife came into the club at various times for their free drinks. Bitt made sure they received excellent service, never waited in line, and, of course, drank free. Chain never caused any trouble. Fortunately, few patrons even noticed that Chain and his wife were there, due to the agreed-upon low-key visitation method.

Bitt was in too many fights to keep track of as he utilized the punching power in his fists of thunder. He typically walked into an opponent and took a shot or two to his head in order to position himself to deliver devastating haymakers. Many of the confrontations were over the dress code, which required a collared shirt. To keep from kicking out too many customers, Bitt would buy collared shirts on sale from JCPenney and keep them in his trunk. Instead of kicking out too many cash-carrying customers, he began practicing some diplomacy and gave them nice new

From Nightlife to Eternal Life

shirts with the price tags still on them. Many of the patrons were pleasantly surprised at Bitt's generosity.

The club generally catered to white customers and became rougher and rougher. The combination of dancing, drinking, music, drugs. and close quarters with a lot of men and women interested in each other for a variety of reasons made for a lot of conflicts. The club was built to hold 150, but there were usually three to four hundred customers present. Many of the physical disagreements were caused by wandering eyes when women or men flirted with someone other than their partner. The crowded conditions made for a powder keg that Bitt and his team were charged with keeping under control. On one occasion, a husband slapped his wife hard enough to knock her down. Bitt put him in a half nelson and dragged him to the door. While he was removing the man, the wife on the receiving end of the punch and her friend were burning Bitt with their cigarette lighters and yelling at him to let her husband go. He pushed the man out the door and handed him over to the off-duty police working security in the parking lot.

Bitt appeared before a local city court judge fifty or more times as a result of customers filing assault charges against him at Stagger Lee's. The person filing the charges didn't show up for the arraignment 95 percent of the time. Bitt experienced a lot of turnover in his bouncer staff. Many were bodybuilders who carried large flashlights, brass knuckles, and slapjacks. Bitt was confident in his toughness to the point of being reckless. He didn't feel the need to carry anything to protect him. His typical team numbered five guys who were all tough. Bitt was now making more than $1,000 a week in salary and cash tips.

CHAPTER 7

Stagger Lee's had run its course and begun to slow down by 1987, when it unceremoniously closed its doors. Other nightspots were gaining in popularity and taking their share of customers in the Atlanta market. Zapf made the most of Stagger Lee's incredibly lucrative, albeit brief, run. Zapf was a frugal man and ran all of his businesses, including his biscuit store and liquor store, tightly and profitably. There had been a lot of violence and many lawsuits, most of them frivolous, filed against the club. Bitt was one of the regulars at the courthouse on Monday mornings to face charges that were usually dismissed when the complaining parties didn't show up. By this time, Bitt had become numb to violence. He'd learned that he had no fear and would take on as many as five or six opponents without a second thought. He had no fear of being bested, and that happened only on rare occasions.

Bitt also cultivated a desire to make big money. But more than money, he wanted power. He had learned how to play the game and how to befriend people. He admired Zapf for exuding power. Zapf was feared and respected and could get about anything he wanted.

Bitt needed a new job and found one utilizing his experience at Big Star Grocery and the Farmer's Market. He worked for about two years for Armor Food Company. He started as a lugger at first, loading and unloading trucks. He was strong and could unload trucks faster than his coworkers. He worked hard and eventually became a shop steward and then a union foreman. He continued to hustle for extra money by selling parlay cards for betting on sporting events. When he became a foreman, he was able to set up arrangements to move contraband with Armor trucks. He continued dabbling in drugs, primarily by bringing together suppliers and pushers. He took a cut off of the top of these transactions. He also cultivated connections with Haitian and Jamaican drug runners he'd first met while transporting grass from the Bahamas to Florida by speedboat with his Sunshine State friend.

He met an underworld character by the name of Rex

Davenport. Bitt utilized the Armor trucks to run product when he drove delivery routes. He would back his truck up to a designated Atlanta warehouse or other location not on the Armor schedule. Anywhere from twenty to forty boxes of contraband would be loaded into it. Bitt would then drop off the boxes at another stop and resume his legitimate deliveries to Armor customers. His customary take for this activity was $1,000 per drop. This was normally a weekly activity, and Bitt eventually learned that the boxes he couriered contained drugs and counterfeit cash. Bitt also met cocaine suppliers through Davenport. He referred them to buyers, primarily his former coworkers and colleagues in the nightclub business. He would earn royalties on these deals, generally $1,000 to $2,000 each time a buy was made. His cash envelopes were delivered without fail so the buyers wouldn't get on the wrong side of Davenport.

The illegal product runs weren't the only black deliveries he made while working at Armor. He also loaded the trucks he drove with extra food and made side deliveries to friends and businesses in the food industry. He sold these food products at deeply discounted prices and pocketed the monies. His services even included the preparation of handwritten generic invoices for his customers to use for tax purposes. He found many small-restaurant patrons willing to partake of his discounted offers. He made significantly more money in his side activities than his official $3,000 monthly Armor salary. Of course, he had expenses. He paid the truck loaders up to $200 to load more food onto their trucks than was necessary for legitimate deliveries.

The money wasn't as important to Bitt as the thrill of being involved in an increasingly high-risk, high-reward lifestyle. However, the money would soon become more of a factor, as he was generous with it on many occasions with family and friends over the years. He continued to collect parlay card bets for a bookie to bump his earnings. He was soon making six figures a year in addition to his Armor salary.

The truth of the matter was that there was a lot of hustling going on at Armor. Many of the workers in addition to Bitt took food at various times. There were always things missing, such as boxes of beef that ended up on the dinner tables of Armor employees. There were a lot of diligent workers who worked hard and never crossed the line, but as many as half of the workforce helped themselves periodically. Armor management suspected they were being taken advantage of and hired a detective to investigate.

The investigation office was set up across the street, and Bitt got wind of it. Before long, Bitt arranged to pay off the detective to keep the heat off of him and the other workers who were liberating boxes of meat. The payoff cost him about $300 a week, and he considered it a cost of doing business.

Bitt's demise at Armor was orchestrated by an ex-neighbor, Lee Collier, who had previously bitten off his wife's nose one night at Brandie's, a Stagger Lee's competitor. Collier was in upper management at Cracker Barrel and had given Bitt a Cracker Barrel Gold Card. This item allowed the bearer and his guests to eat free at any Cracker Barrel in the United States. Bitt used it a lot and also loaned it out to friends. Collier was fired by Cracker Barrel for a drug problem. He opened his own restaurant and regularly teamed up with Bitt to move counterfeit money and engage in other under-the-surface activities. Bitt, nudged by Cindy, his materialistic wife, was starting to accumulate nice clothes and expensive cars. He was living in Point South, an upscale neighborhood in Jonesboro, Georgia, at the time.

Collier let Bitt down in a counterfeit-money scheme. Bitt knew of some Haitian buyers who were interested in buying high-quality paper to make funny money. Rex Davenport had referred the would-be paper buyers to Bitt, and that was all he knew and needed to know about them. They were serious players and had plenty of legitimate cash to buy what they wanted. Collier and Bitt discussed the matter and decided they would supply a high grade of paper to close the deal and make a nice profit. Bitt felt confident because Collier had come up with quality paper on previous occasions. A meeting to consummate the deal was held in the freezer at Collier's restaurant, a converted Huddle House. A payoff of up to $100,000 was likely if the buyers were pleased. It quickly became apparent that the paper Collier was trying to sell was of extremely poor quality. The dreadlocked Haitian trio was upset and let it be known. Bitt was able to soothe their ruffled feathers, and the Haitians left without buying any of the paper but, more importantly, without taking their pound of flesh for their time being wasted.

Although he should have been grateful for being extricated from a potentially deadly situation, Collier harbored a grudge against Bitt for the deal having gone sour. Bitt had also referred him to buyers for profitable paper deals in the past. Collier proceeded to write a letter to Armor and inform them that Bitt was selling him meat products for greatly discounted prices. He even attached copies of invoices Bitt had given him to document the transactions for tax purposes. Needless to say, Armor was not happy to learn of Bitt's extracurricular activities. Armor management called Bitt in and invited him to resign. They also informed him that they had been investigating their inventory shortages for quite some time. Bitt resigned as requested.

CHAPTER 8

Within a week, Bitt was employed at the Gold Club in Atlanta. He landed a security position through his friend Taylor Bishop. Bitt and Bishop played weekend softball with a team that included a couple of high-level players who also worked at the Gold Club. Bitt was an aggressive, brash player, as evidenced by his unorthodox pitching style. He would often loft a slow pitch to the batter and then charge toward the batter's box. He also threw his glove off and played bare-handed a lot. On one occasion, he borrowed a glove from an opponent's young son, who was sitting in the dugout. He could barely fit his hand into it, but he used it during the entire contest. Bitt was as abrasive as he was good in softball at that point in his life, and he thoroughly enjoyed himself.

David and Pat Patterson were minority owners of the Gold

Club, and they attended many games of the team their business sponsored. When Bitt was playing his first game with Bishop, the Patterson brothers pulled into the ballpark parking lot in a limousine with several of the club's dancers in tow. The Gold Club team finished as runners-up that weekend in the restaurant and bar tournament before large crowds at the Country Club Softball Complex. The Pattersons enjoyed walking out to the mound and conferring with Bitt in the same manner a major-league baseball pitching coach did. Bitt played along and stoked their egos by asking them what they wanted him to do. They told him they liked it when he charged the batter's box after releasing a pitch. They also liked it when he tossed his glove in the air and played bare-handed. Bitt eventually developed a pitch in which he placed the ball in his glove with his hat on top of it. He perfected a routine in which he tossed all three up in the air together. Unbelievably, the hat would veer one way, the glove would veer the other way, and the ball would magically cross the center of plate in a graceful loop. This was the type of showmanship the Pattersons loved, and they jumped at the chance to hire Bitt as a bouncer when Bishop suggested it to them. His buddy Sam Watterson also worked there.

The Gold Club was started with $100,000 investments from

twenty-one individuals. This paid for the property and built the building. The twenty-one names were listed on the front of the club's safe. Each investor was guaranteed $135,000 after one year and $165,000 after two years. Beginning with the third year, the investors were guaranteed a proportionate percentage of stock (about 5 percent) if they weren't repaid their original investment and the targeted surplus. The Pattersons tracked the repayment of the investors and marked off their names as they were repaid. Soon only the Pattersons and Cliff Eggers remained as owners and investors, although the Pattersons didn't invest their own money. Bitt was to become a close friend of Eggers, who soon became the majority owner.

The Gold Club started off slowly. It was associated with Don Ferr, the owner of the Million Dollar Saloon in Dallas, Texas. The dancers at the Gold Club were beautiful but were topless only, as were their counterparts in Dallas. Bitt determined that the Gold Club had a problem. It didn't have nude dancers, only topless ones. Bitt shook the bushes at the corporate offices in Dallas by sending in a fax requesting a complete football uniform for each of the club employees. This prompted an angry call from Eggers in Dallas. He asked for Bitt and wanted to know more about his crazy fax. Bitt told him in no uncertain terms that the Gold Club desperately needed to employ completely nude dancers to compete with the other local nightspots. Furthermore, Bitt told him, if they couldn't have them, he needed to put all of the club employees in football uniforms to knock down and tackle the customers to keep them in the club when they saw it providing only topless dancing. Eggers said he'd think about it and call him back. He did so a couple hours later and said he was flying to Atlanta in two days. He asked Bitt to pick him up.

Another of Bitt's side ventures was partial ownership interest in a limousine firm. He picked up Eggers in a limo and had three party girls with him. He dropped Eggers off at a luxury hotel in Buckhead, the upscale Atlanta community. He didn't hear from him until a couple of days later. He asked Bitt to pick him up and make his case for changing the club's policy on nudity. He only had a couple of hours before he was going to fly back to Dallas. Bitt decided to show him some local clubs with inferior amenities that outperformed the Gold Club using nude dancers. He took him to several. All were full of customers despite neon-lit fronts, bad sound systems, and ratty, worn-out furnishings. He told Eggers that the Gold Club was a state-of-the-art facility but wouldn't draw more customers without full nudity. He reminded him that Atlanta was a big convention city. A week later, the Gold Club introduced nude dancing.

A short time later, Taylor Bishop was fired after a disagreement with the Pattersons. A vociferous bodybuilder, Bishop was outspoken like Bitt and wouldn't back down. As a result, Bitt became the club manager two months after being hired. He sought the approval of his friend Bishop, who told him to take the job, as he was already lined up elsewhere. Bitt began by putting some innovative practices in place. He made friends with the other limo services in Atlanta and the cab drivers. He offered them complimentary drinks for the night if they suggested the Gold Club to their fares looking for a little excitement. The limo drivers and cabbies were also allowed to bring their friends with them for the free drinks.

The Gold Club became a place to be seen. Athletes, celebrities, and political power brokers were constant customers. The dancers were top notch and, of course, nude. They pushed Gold Bucks, which were sold to customers with a 10 percent surcharge. They also gave customers cash from credit card advances, but Bitt knew that customers would spend Gold Bucks like Monopoly money.

Psychologically, they were much more likely to hang on to their twenty-dollar bills, but they parted with Gold Bucks much more freely. The club charged the 10 percent surcharge to the customers who used them to pay the dancers and waitresses for their lap dances and drinks. At the end of their shifts, when the girls turned in the Gold Bucks they'd collected, management paid them 90 percent of what they turned in, making a total of 20 percent in the exchange. Dancers and waitresses were allowed to keep cash tips received directly from customers for drinks, dances, and hanging out with them. However, the majority of the patrons enjoyed buying and distributing Gold Bucks.

Additionally, Bitt and the other club staffers trained the dancers and waitresses to go slow and treat the customers nicely. Drink servers always asked the customers if they wanted to buy their temporary female companion a drink, which they almost always did. The dancers were allowed to offer lap dances, and they were trained to tell the customer they liked him but had to move on to make more money during their shifts. As one might expect, the customers often pulled out more Gold Bucks and asked the dancers to remain in their company instead of moving on.

The club kept growing as it brought in more and more beautiful dancers. They soon had shifts of seventy dancers. The waitresses and hostesses in the crowd took turns dancing in the buff and were scantily clad off stage, often in expensive lingerie. Management wanted a sexy but not slutty look. The loud music was provided by a number of prominent entertainment disc jockeys, including Jeff Nair. Local radio deejays were also hired, and they worked at the club during the hours they weren't on air. They also provided the club with free advertising, as they would promote their Gold Club shifts to their listeners and encourage them to patronize the club. Bitt and management used this strategy, among others, to spread the word about the Gold Club, and it worked.

Bitt's salary was structured with bonuses based on total gross receipts. At first, he received a bonus if the club had a $30,000 week. Within six months of starting at the Gold Club, Bitt was blowing up the $30,000 goal. The club was drawing a lot of convention business because of the nude dancers. Atlanta's city government was uncomfortable with the total nudity and began working to bring back only topless dancers to the nightclub industry. Bitt believed this problem shifted a significant amount of convention business to Las Vegas, where total nudity was the norm. The Gold Club was a favorite hot spot for about forty national conventions, which whittled down to five as the convention business shifted to Vegas.

Bitt made a noteworthy mistake before going to work for the Gold Club. He went to a club known for being a dope-slinging establishment. Taylor Bishop, one of his closest friends and a conservative tough guy, was working there at the time. He was in the habit of splurging on a big birthday bash for himself every year. In 1987, Bishop called Bitt, who was planning to come to the party. It was being held on the entire floor of an upscale hotel. Bishop told Bitt that some of the partygoers were interested in scoring some cocaine. Bitt had kept his drug connections quiet, but he considered Bishop a true friend, so he took his personal stash, a quarter kilo of cocaine, and proceeded to bust it open. He then wrapped it up and drove it to the party in his Corvette.

A lot of customers of Bishop's current employer were present for the three-day extravaganza. There were areas in the hotel furnished with sectional couches and other lounge chairs for the comfort of the friends of Bishop, including many athletes, musicians, and entertainers. Bitt delivered the coke as requested but then made a big mistake: he placed the big chunk of cocaine on the table for the partygoers. Bishop immediately snatched it up and took it into a bedroom because he didn't want everybody present to know about it. Several people saw Bitt bring the dope and soon made a practice of hounding him for more, remembering his delivery and display long afterward. On the bright side, he then had his choice of girls who were impressed with his ability to produce so much cocaine at one time. On the not-so-bright side, he soon had to move because of so many unwanted visitors and callers looking to buy from him at all hours of the day and night.

His first year at the Gold Club was successful for him from an earnings standpoint. Bitt made a lot of money by spending it to make it. Now in the limousine business, he typically had one of his drivers take him in a stretch limo to the club for his shifts. He would get out of the vehicle and hand the two to three valets on duty $100 apiece. He slipped the door girls $200 each. Now everyone handling the arriving customers was greased. Bitt received tips from most of the employees for leading customers to their stations. He took in frequent twenty-five-dollar tips from the bartenders and at least ten-dollar periodic payments from the waitresses. The dancers tipped 10 percent of their cash tips to the deejay, who shared the money with Bitt and his staff. The dancers also gave Bitt anywhere from ten to a hundred dollars for pointing customers their way when they left the stage. Within an hour and a half, Bitt would recover his initial $500 to $700 investment on arrival, and then it was gravy for the rest of the night.

Trying to avoid unwanted visitors and callers wanting drugs, he moved into a hotel, the Ramada Renaissance, for a temporary place to hide out before finding a new house. He ended up staying in the hotel's Jimmy Carter Suite for eighteen months. He worked out a deal and paid fifty dollars a night for three connected rooms. He put his driver in one of them and, doing a favor for a friend, offered the third room to a recently released felon. It happened to be Billy Carter, who had been a star basketball player at the University of North Carolina. Down the road, Billy, Bishop, and Bitt would face legal problems together in Florida because Carter would run his mouth.

Bitt was receiving a lot of cash and gift cards from Gold Club customers for retail stores and restaurants. One customer, Wally Bishop, was a real-estate developer who owned a couple of upscale Marietta eateries. Bitt took a date to one of his places and was conservative in his spending, totaling about $120. As promised by Bishop, he was comped on the bill. Bishop came into the Gold Club soon after and tossed down the receipt of the expense for

Bitt's recent evening. He acted insulted and instructed Bitt to come back the next chance he had, spend some "real money," and have a good time with his girl. Bishop routinely picked up Gold Club dancers so he and his friends could take them out and party. He often took them to local clothing stores and bought them expensive dresses as part of the deal.

Bitt returned to Bishop's place a few nights later and decided to take him up on his invitation. He ordered a bottle of Moët White Star champagne for every table in the restaurant. He figured this might irritate Bishop, but he didn't care and was anxious to see his reaction. Bishop came into the club a few nights later. He slapped Bitt on the back, showed him the receipt for his recent visit, and told him, "Now, this is what I'm talking about when I tell you to have a good time." Bitt estimated the bill was $2,000 to $3,000. He gave the waiters a $300 tip. Bishop frequently rented out one of the private rooms at the Gold Club for himself and his guys. The rent was buying a minimum of one bottle of Dom Pérignon champagne per hour to keep the room and the girls for his group. Of course, lots of cash and Gold Bucks were spent.

The Gold Club was such a popular place that Bitt and some of his colleagues were given free designer suits and clothing to allow merchants to come in and drink for free. The quality of the dancers was top flight. The club was so popular and the dancers were so beautiful that *Playboy* included seventeen of them in their first lingerie issue. Hugh Hefner asked for permission for his magazine staff to come into the club, observe, and select some for inclusion in the special edition.

All of the dancers at the Gold Club worked for tips only. Much as Bitt paid fellow employees and received cash from the same, the dancers shared their tips with other club employees who supported the structure, allowing for them to meet customers willing to part with their cash and Gold Bucks. Bitt and his staff kept several activity sheets for the dancers to help track the tips and prevent skimming. There were lists at the door and the bar and one kept with the house mother. It was a tipping business. The dancers would track the results of other dancers and try to out-tip each other with respect to the deejay, the security team, and other employees. Some of the dancers made net proceeds between $1,000 and $2,000 a night.

Bitt found out that many of the beautiful dancers would come on to the club employees, patrons, or anyone willing to give them cash. As a result, he made efforts to avoid becoming involved with the girls working in the club. He made one notable exception to this self-imposed rule. He fell in love with a beautiful California dancer, Betty Duncan, who was studying international medicine. Her sister Sandy was an attorney and also performed. They flew to Atlanta once a month to dance for the weekend, make some cash, and experience life on the wild side. Bitt was smitten with both of the sisters, particularly Betty. One night, Betty told Bitt that her sister had a crush on him. Bitt replied that he thought Sandy was the second most beautiful girl in the building. He further told Betty that he had a crush on someone else, and she was standing right next to him, although he had been too shy to approach her. She looked at him and said, "I'm engaged." However, the next month, Betty returned to the club by herself. She oozed class as far as Bitt was concerned, and she decided to stay with him instead of returning to her studies in Denmark. She skipped a semester of medical school, and they lived together for six months.

Bitt figured Betty wanted a little trip down the other side. Betty and her sister each made $5,000 to $10,000 during three-day weekends dancing at the club. The Gold Club offered a little bit of unorganized gambling activity. Bitt, some of the employees, and a few customers loved pitching quarters for anywhere from fifty to a hundred dollars per throw. Betty eventually tired of gambling with her future and patched up things with her fiancé. She left the Gold Club spotlight experience and went back to him. Bitt was not particularly upset. He had always believed she was on a temporary fling and would tire of the notoriety of performing in front of celebrities and sports stars. The likes of Rod Stewart would come in and be treated like any other customer due to the club's incredible popularity. The Gold Club categorized celebrities as A list and B list. A-listers received one free bottle of Dom, and B-listers were given a free bottle of Moët. The club had to eventually build outside storage areas and coolers in order to keep enough liquor on hand.

Bitt was known as a kingpin drug dealer by the DEA and local law enforcement. It was an incorrect assumption, since he was only dabbling in cocaine for occasional personal use and wasn't pushing it or setting up any serious deals. He snorted coke every month or two, but it never became habit forming. He had connections with big-time drug dealers throughout the country but didn't utilize them for business purposes at the time. He was making $65,000 to $70,000 in wages but brought in close to a million dollars a year in tips, most of which he spent on himself, his friends, and greasing palms. He was working five nights a week but drank only sparingly. He made exceptions for some of the local professional athletes, several of whom were members of the Atlanta Braves. He also shared an occasional drink with sports suppliers, such as Nike and the likes of Magic Johnson and Michael Jordan.

Betty's departure didn't bother Bitt, and he immediately replaced her with another beauty he met at the club, Rosey Benson. After being with a lady of movie-star stature for a while, Bitt found Rosey to be a breath of fresh air. An occasional patron and not a dancer, she was a good-looking southern girl, and she moved to Florida with Bitt after his time with the Gold Club. He later regretted letting her get away. Bitt eventually walked away from an impressive list of acquaintances from his time with the Gold Club, including Metallica, Def Leppard, Guns and Roses, Lawrence Taylor, and Hank Williams Jr., to name just a few. Bitt estimated that at least 50 percent of the NBA, NFL, and MLB patronized the club. It was one of the most popular spots in the country.

Bitt experienced second thoughts and regrets about his life for the first time a couple of months before his run at the Gold Club would end. He woke up in the middle of the night to find himself alone in a big, dark hotel room. In that quiet vacuum, he felt lost and dead. He knew he was missing something in life beyond regular sleep. He acknowledged to himself that he had gotten away from all of the good things in his life, including God, softball, family, and wholesome, grounded females. He packed up his suits and loaded them into his red Corvette. He took the ever-present Gideon hotel Bible with him and headed back to LaGrange to his parents' house. He began to ask himself, "How am I going to approach my mother and father now?" He drove for more than an hour and reached the exit leading to his childhood home. However, feeling ashamed and lost, he turned around and drove back to Atlanta and the Monday morning managers' meeting at the club. Later that day, he checked back into the Ramada. He figured he was paving his path straight to hell, but he wasn't ready to take a detour yet. His first small step to redemption was still a few years away.

CHAPTER 9

In 1989, Bitt had exceeded all expectations of the Pattersons for the Gold Club. However, his demise in the business started one night when he made a questionable decision. He allowed a friend to close a two-kilo cocaine deal in the parking lot of the club. He then allowed the dealer to count his take in Bitt's office. Shortly after it was confirmed that the selling price of $62,000 had been delivered in small bills, the Pattersons walked into the room. They asked where the money had come from, and Bitt arrogantly responded, "Would you believe a big night in tips?" He then asked them to leave and shut the door behind them. This convinced the Pattersons that Bitt was out of control. He had earned the loyalty of the night staff and his general manager and superior, Sam Watterson, who'd come over from a competing club. Watterson tried to keep Bitt under control to no avail.

Watterson unknowingly did Bitt a favor when he hired Tim Morrison of Cumming, Georgia, as a bouncer. Morrison reported to Bitt, and they became close lifelong friends after Morrison impressed Bitt early in his tenure at the Gold Club. He threw a rowdy patron off of the stairway landing into the lobby area, where he landed at Bitt's feet. Bitt was impressed with Morrison's actions and made him his right-hand man in the club. Morrison, a married man, appreciated Bitt pressing hundred-dollar bills into his palm on a regular basis. Morrison witnessed many occasions when Bitt choked out unruly customers, and during one such event, Bitt dragged the culprit in front of a floor-length mirror so he could watch himself pass out. Morrison also saw Bitt explain the touch-and-go policy to a busload of former South Carolina football players. He boarded the bus and told the crowd, which numbered more than forty, that if they touched a girl, they would be forced to go. After being struck in the head by a flying beer bottle, Bitt attempted to fight everyone on the bus. Morrison and other Gold Club associates had to pull him off the bus so it could leave the parking lot and find another entertainment spot. Decades later, Bitt would be a positive influence on Morrison in the spiritual realm, but that was still far down the road.

An exotic dancer, Jeannie, was a well-known and popular adult female entertainer in Atlanta. She became good friends with Bitt. Jeannie thought she was destined to move to Hollywood with Rod Stewart. She and Bitt respected each other for their work ethic and drive. She lived in an upscale Atlanta apartment complex, the Art Towers. She suggested Bitt consider moving into the Towers to be closer to downtown for more marketing opportunities. The only unit available was the penthouse apartment. Bitt had no idea the Pattersons also lived in the complex. They saw Bitt on the elevator when he was checking out the top floor. This coincidence, along with the pile of money they had recently viewed on his desk at the club, made them uneasy and even more suspicious of Bitt. Little did they know that the rent for the penthouse was less than Bitt shelled out each month for the Jimmy Carter Suite at the Ramada.

All of the original investors in the Gold Club had recovered their investments and made tidy profits by that time. The remaining owners were now Eggers and the Pattersons. Eggers was a 51 percent shareholder. The Pattersons were rumored to own small clubs in Dallas and spent limited time in Atlanta, but they made a lot of money, as the club often pulled in $40,000 per night and sometimes more. Bitt was the key to the success of the business and called most of the shots, greasing the wheels of the enterprise. He continued to maintain the peace whenever necessary and faced off daunting numbers of inebriated customers many times. On one occasion, Bitt was fighting in the parking lot with rowdy bachelor party patrons he had kicked out for poor behavior. He was dragged into the open door of a limousine, and it drove off. Soon he was being dragged down the street with his legs dangling out and under the vehicle's frame. Bitt was punching his way out of things, when the limo wrecked. Bitt, Morrison, and a couple of other Gold Club employees then dragged the occupants out of the limo and schooled them.

Most of the time, customers caused trouble by trying to grope the dancers and waitresses. Morrison was especially valuable to Bitt, as he could knock down abusive customers with thunderous punches as opposed to Bitt's choke-'em-out routine. Many of the misbehaving customers were outlandish and not receptive to Bitt's attempts at making peace. One particularly big fight involved Bitt, Morrison, the rest of the security crew, and other employees against twenty-five to thirty out-of-control bachelor party attendees. It took only a few minutes for the offenders to be dispatched to the parking lot. Many of the other patrons stood on tables and the bar to view the action. At the conclusion of the incident, the deejay screamed into his microphone, "We work in the Gold Club! It's not just a job; it's an adventure!" There was gigantic applause in response to his shout-out. The club's reputation grew, and Bitt was a huge part of it.

The Gold Club, in an approach similar to the one used by Stagger Lee's, catered to a higher-class crowd with expensive clothes and money to burn. Still, a dope dealer with snakeskin boots and a T-shirt could buy his way in with a C-note for the door girl and willingness to buy a bottle of champagne. Bitt, wearing his own expensive clothes, walked up and down the line of two hundred to three hundred waiting to get into the club with a leather-bound notebook and asked people how many were in their party. He didn't care for an answer, but this activity would draw those with a lot of disposable cash in their pockets to ask how they might buy their way in ahead of everyone else. Bitt always responded, "Anything can be expedited for a man of your means." Bitt wouldn't let a dope boy and his crew in one night because they weren't properly dressed. The leader popped a razor out and sliced Bitt's thumb. Bitt retaliated by punching him one time with each fist, grabbing him by the neck, and wrapping a nearby phone booth cord around his neck to squeeze it. While this lesson was being taught, a couple of rock-star celebrities walked by and high-fived him.

This was during the era of increasing cocaine use, but the Gold Club tried not to cater to the new breed of users. Meanwhile, the Pattersons decided that Bitt had to go. He was too popular and, frankly, too powerful for their liking. They hired a new night manager named Dan. His first night on the job, Bitt and the rest of the team were chasing a record night of $50,000 in receipts. Jeff Patterson and Dan were close friends. Dan had worked for him in one of the Pattersons' Dallas nightspots. Bitt had an operational routine in place in which waitresses greeted and seated customers, took their orders, and got them acclimated quickly. The entire staff was excited about the possibility of having a record money-breaking night.

Jeff Patterson and Dan were drinking heavily and started to cause trouble for their own staff. They would wad up napkins, throw them down, and then ask Bitt why there was trash on the floor. The first couple of times, Bitt didn't realize what was going on and had the waitresses pick them up. He even picked up a few himself. After seeing what was going on, he went to their table and called them children. He said he was going for a record and the $1,000 bonus it would net him. He then proceeded to tell the two that if they didn't behave, he would throw them out of the club with no regard for the fact that one of them was an owner. He further told them that the team was pushing for a record, and they needed to stay out of the way. This dressing down took place in front of several of the staff.

The next night, Dan came into the club, and Bitt was directed to give him anything he wanted. Dan immediately began bothering the female dancers and employees. Bitt went to him and told him to stop. Bitt explained that he didn't know how things worked in Dallas, but the Gold Club took care of its female employees. He delivered the message in a respectful manner and told Dan he was aware that he was a special guest of the Pattersons, but he needed to refrain from touching the girls. Another incident took place a short time later, and Morrison was directed to bring Dan to Bitt's office. When he entered, Bitt told him he needed to leave the club, and he was giving him the opportunity to walk out peacefully.

Bitt and Dan walked out of the office, and the visitor quickly grabbed at the first girl who walked by them. Bitt had seen enough and proceeded to remove Dan from the premises. He dragged him down the stairs to the main floor. He rubbed his face on one side of the stucco walls of the first flight and then scraped his face on the other side on the second flight. As a result, Dan's face was injured on both sides. Bitt wanted the girls in the club to see what happened to someone who mistreated them. Outside the club, Dan came after Bitt, who dropped him like a sack of potatoes and then put him in a cab. A short time later, Dan returned to the club with a gun. That was a big mistake. Bitt worked him over, breaking his jaw and several of his ribs. He took care of Dan that night, but he realized that his days at the Gold Club were numbered. Three months later, Dan healed up, returned, and took Bitt's job.

Bitt was fired when he refused to submit to a urinalysis at the weekly 8:00 a.m. managers' meeting. That was not a routine procedure. He was replaced by Jeff Patterson's buddy Dan. Bitt was used to being a VIP in the Atlanta scene and used his club management experience to quickly land a South Florida job with Jack Davidson, who owned more than fifty nightclubs across the country. While making a cold-call visit to Davidson's office, Bitt was hired to oversee Pure Platinum, Solid Gold, and the Doll House in the Fort Lauderdale area. His salesmanship and outgoing demeanor again served him well. He shared a home for a short time with nightclub comedian Jay Hickman, the Duke of Dirt, but within a couple of weeks, Bitt began to miss his Georgia friends, and he also still had clothing and belongings in Atlanta. He decided to return to see his buddies for a weekend reunion only a few weeks after his Gold Club termination.

He drove straight through to Atlanta and went to the Gold Club to say goodbye to everyone. He settled in at the bar, and all of the employees and some of the customers treated him like the prodigal son. He was throwing down complimentary drinks and hugging friends and former coworkers, when Dan learned he was in the club. From his office, Dan called Morrison, who was still on the payroll, and told him to throw Bitt out. Morrison told Dan that if he wanted Bitt ejected, he could do it himself. None of the other security staff would agree to toss out Bitt either, especially if it went against Morrison's wishes. Bitt was the king again for a few hours. He went so far as to start semimanaging the club operations again, perhaps due to nostalgia and his love for the employees and friends. He didn't care that he wasn't being paid. He even went so far as to assist in balancing the receipts in the cash registers with the bartenders.

Dan remained in his office the entire night to avoid Bitt, who was dusted and drunk. When he came out to begin the closing process, Dan said something to Bitt that he didn't clearly hear or understand. In any event, Bitt jumped at him and started a shoving match. A couple of bouncers pulled Bitt off of Dan, but in the process, Bitt managed to twist Dan's wrist and grab the keys to the safe. He quickly stuffed them in his pocket. Now Dan had no way to lock up the nightly receipts, although he didn't know it yet. After drinking and snorting some cocaine, counting out the night's money, confronting Dan, and grabbing his keys, Bitt snatched up a fifth of whiskey and left for a nearby Waffle House. It was between four and five o'clock in the morning, and he was hungry after such a busy night.

There were few other customers in the restaurant other than some professional wrestlers. They helped Bitt drink the whiskey. The front door to the Waffle House opened, and in walked Morrison with several police officers, including the watch commander. He knew Bitt and greeted him. Bitt stood up and shook his hand as if they were greeting each other at any social event. He smiled and asked the commander how he was doing. The response was "Gee, Bitt, I didn't know they were pouring in the Waffle House now" as he stared at the whiskey bottle on the table in the booth.

Bitt said they did so on certain occasions. When the commander asked if this was one of those occasions, Bitt replied, "It is if you want it to be, sir."

Ignoring his reply, the commander said, "Please tell me you don't have the Gold Club manager's keys. He can't get into the safe room."

Bitt replied, "The keys to what, sir?"

The commander responded, "Bitt."

Bitt immediately said, "Yes, sir, I have them." When asked why he took the keys, Bitt remarked, "I really don't know. I was reaching for the manager and was going to take him outside with me, and I ended up with the keys." When asked to produce the keys, Bitt complied and said, "Sure, anything for you, sir."

Bitt slept at a local hotel and headed back to Florida after he woke up. He stayed at the Ramada since he was persona non grata at the Buckhead Embassy Hotel after a wild night several months earlier. Driving south, he came to the stark realization that he was still addicted to the fast lifestyle of money changing hands and celebrities hobnobbing with him. He loved the thrills, the power, and the interaction with famous people. He hoped to find these things in Florida. He would find them and more in the coming months.

CHAPTER 10

He returned to Fort Lauderdale and began to improve the profit margin in Davidson's clubs in many ways. Bitt was cocky and recognized that the atmosphere in the three local joints was stiff. There were no vibes. Davidson told Bitt that he'd graduated first in his class at Cornell before he came to Orlando for the purpose of becoming a gangster. He dressed like Kevin Costner in the well-known movie *Bull Durham*, and Bitt thought of his wardrobe as "a little excessive for the Carolina League." Davidson further explained to Bitt that he'd gone to work for a Florida tennis and racquetball country club and made it successful through hard work. He'd lived on the grounds but worked himself out of a job by making the business profitable. The owner had sold it after about a year. But Davidson had received a bonus for saving the property from going under and making it something of value.

To celebrate his cash influx, he'd gone to a local strip club. He'd noticed that this particular establishment was lacking in class.

He had paid the cover charge and bought an overpriced drink. The diminutive Davidson had thought about what the club might do if it was cleaned up and made classier. Before long, he and Jack Jonesboro had opened the Doll House in Fort Lauderdale. It featured a clean environment, well-dressed dancers, and personable employees. However, Bitt noticed that neither the Doll House nor the other Davidson clubs had private rooms, which his experience told him would lead to big champagne sales. Bitt's first managers' meeting in the Davidson organization didn't win him any friends. One employee for Davidson, known as Duke, was a former DEA employee who'd helped his boss out of a jam while still working for the DEA. Rumor had it that some evidence against Davidson had "disappeared," and Duke had soon retired from the DEA and gone to work for Davidson. Duke immediately recognized that Bitt was a criminal and told him so. He also advised Bitt that his look and demeanor would draw attention from local law enforcement. He cautioned Bitt not to trust anyone in South Florida, but unfortunately, Bitt didn't heed that advice down the road.

During his first managers' meeting, Bitt told Davidson and his management staff that they were running backward. This comment was not received well. He went on to explain that their clubs were too stiff, and there was not enough fun going on. He said the clubs were also too bright, and there was no incentive to sell champagne. He added that there were no private rooms to push champagne and encourage big spenders to let go of their money. Jack Jonesboro was present and went to see Bitt the next day during his day shift at Pure Platinum. He recognized that Bitt had a point. He gave Bitt the authority to improve Pure Platinum any way he saw fit. Bitt changed the look of the club by painting the panels on the ceiling purple, installing string lights, and building four private rooms. Bitt also made the club friendlier by instructing the employees to greet customers and make them feel important. The receipts soon began to climb steadily, due in large part to Bitt's personality and likeability.

One of the co-owners of Pure Platinum called Bitt on the phone about an expense that he noticed incurred in the club. He chastised Bitt for buying and giving away $100 worth of cigars to customers. He had no idea that local club competitors were already offering Bitt jobs. The part owner, Brad Andrews, went to Pure

Jim Henninger

Platinum and observed a group of former Miami Dolphins in one of the private rooms. They were drinking Moët through straws, partying with club girls, and smoking cigars provided by Bitt. He realized a good thing when he saw it, and he told Bitt to proceed with his management style. Davidson was grooming Bitt to be the general manager of his soon-to-be newly licensed club, Solid Gold of Miami. The plan was to open an all-nude facility when the local permits were secured. Bitt and Davidson planned to bring in the most beautiful dancers in the Davidson clubs from around the country, a successful strategy he had followed in the past. As the business grew, Bitt was going to hire local girls and replace the A team of dancers in stages over time. To no one's surprise, Bitt's announced promotion wasn't popular with the rest of Davidson's management staff. Bitt was privately considering arranging another round of group breast enhancements for the dancers, similar to what he'd cooked up with a local plastic surgeon in Atlanta. Of course, the girls would sign personal service contracts and pay back the surgical fees over time. Bitt's clubs always made money in every way possible.

Several of Bitt's acquaintances followed him to Florida to the land of milk and honey. This group consisted of Billy Carter,

Scott Alvarez, Tom Osteen, and a few others. Osteen specialized in selling crystal meth. They were all drug dealers with whom Bitt had dabbled in a few deals in Atlanta. Primarily, Bitt put buyers, such as Carter, together with suppliers for a finder's fee. They had moved a lot of cocaine in Georgia and relocated to Florida for more opportunities and greater profit margins. They figured Bitt could put them in touch with southern suppliers, and they were right. He still had his contacts with the group he'd helped distribute contraband while working at Armor in Atlanta. One of the transplanted associates, Carter, would contribute heavily to Bitt's eventual arrest on drug charges.

Bitt was biding his time for six to eight months while waiting for the paperwork to be wrapped up prior to the opening of the Miami club. He struggled to make Pure Platinum more viable during the daytime, which was usually slow. He decided to make the club look cozier by installing a curtain, thereby making the space seem much smaller. He knew this would make Platinum appear busier and more intimate and allow the customers to be closer to the girls dancing and waiting on tables. He also decided to improve the acoustics; he attached a layer of Plexiglas to the ceiling and painted it dark purple. Afterward, he hung Christmas lights to make it look like the nighttime sky. He also put in VIP rooms with dividers for three-walled areas. Each room was near the dressing room, so the users could watch the girls walk into and out of it. Bitt knew the rooms would be hugely popular and would spike champagne sales. Bitt bought couches to put in the rooms. This idea took off so well that it spilled over into the evenings. He also suggested that all of the waitresses be incentivized to sell champagne. Accordingly, the sales of champagne skyrocketed, and the culture changed. The waitresses quickly found out that selling a $300 bottle of champagne made for a much larger tip than pushing beer all night long.

Davidson and Jonesboro assigned Bitt to run Pure Platinum during the day and to visit the other two clubs at night to look for ways to improve their performance. He also went into other popular nightspots and made friends. This led to more walk-in business in the clubs run by Davidson, because the friends Bitt made were coming in to see him at night in response to his patronizing their restaurants and bars. Bitt was sitting in Pure Platinum after his shift had ended one evening, when he noticed former Miami Dolphins quarterback and network TV sports analyst Dan Marino enter. Bitt knew Marino from his time at the Gold Club. He briefly thought to himself that he would never be as happy anywhere as he was during his ride to the top while running the Gold Club in its prime. Marino approached Bitt from behind and bear-hugged him to the surprise of the employees and patrons. He wanted to know what Bitt was doing in Fort Lauderdale. After a few drinks, they decided to go to the Doll House.

For fun, Bitt also took Marino to Solid Gold, which was the former location of Bachelors III, a club once partially owned by New York Jet great Joe Namath. Not yet open to the public, Solid Gold was nearly finished and ready to go. Bitt took Marino upstairs to an office and asked him if he knew who used to set up shop there. Marino asked if it was Joe Willie, Namath's nickname, and Bitt told him it certainly was. The room was impressive. It was about two thousand square feet, with a snow-white marble bar and white marble floor. It was mob-style in its decor. Marino was impressed and grateful for the chance to see the former nightclub office of the NFL Hall of Famer and former Alabama great.

Bitt was looking forward to assuming the general manager duties at Solid Gold when the permit work was finished. But he would end up being arrested three days before the opening occurred. In recent weeks, Bitt had introduced several dope boys from Atlanta to suppliers, most of whom were Latinos from Colombia or Cuba. His original connection to these cartels was through a childhood friend from the LaGrange area. He again ran some boats from Bermuda and unloaded some drug-carrying DC-10s that landed on private property in Ocala, Florida. There were approximately twenty people required to quickly unload a DC-10. These activities were organized by a thug calling himself Tia Mahia. The unloading occurred on his horse farm. The boat runs and unloading sessions netted Bitt about $5,000 per event. Bitt also personally introduced his Atlanta visitors to Colombian and Cuban contacts to do business. Several of the Atlanta visitors frequented Club New in the Miami area. It was a popular spot with skyboxes, music, food, drinks, and massive amounts of champagne. Club New was popular with many local celebrities, including Lou Rawls and Julio Iglesias. Bitt conducted business with the blessings of the Colombian and Cuban suppliers he knew. He took his dope boys to Club New, and the suppliers decided whether or not to do business with them. Usually, an arrangement was worked out.

Bitt was on the verge of having access to millions of dollars in the blossoming South Florida drug business of the '90s if he could avoid being arrested or killed. When drug deals were arranged, Bitt's take was $10,000 to $15,000, depending on how many kilos were sold. He was the middleman in countless deals in the first eight months he resided in Florida. The uncut cocaine for sale was highly desired by the Atlanta dealers. Billy Carter, Bitt's old acquaintance, was not selective in his relationships and began working with several crack cocaine dealers. These particular criminals were young, flashy, and aggressive. Bitt set up a few buys for Carter's groups but tired of brokering for the meth dealers. Instead, Bitt took Carter to meet his buyers, as his appearance and demeanor were acceptable.

At Platinum, Bitt ran into a problem with a group who called themselves the Black Death. They were a drug-taking Goth group, and one of them was dating a Platinum waitress. They were not the kind of clientele Bitt wanted or allowed in Platinum. After they displayed disrespect to him, Bitt kicked out a group of them, roughing them up in the process. One pulled a gun out of his car and pointed it at Bitt in the parking lot. Bitt told him, "That's the biggest mistake you've ever made. I'll get you no matter how long it takes me." It didn't take long. Bitt chased the gun-toting young man to a nearby hotel parking lot. After a short pursuit from there, Bitt caught him on a rooftop and hammered him. To Bitt's surprise, he had visitors in his rental house before he came home that night.

Upon arriving at home, he found his half of the rental house unlocked, and several dead, gutted cats were hanging throughout his place. Some of them were gracing a ceiling fan. Bitt had quite a mess to clean up. He had to arrange for new sheet rock because of the absorbed fluids and resultant odor. Lucky for the Black Death, who were all Caucasians, Bitt was arrested before he found any of them. The waitress who was supposedly dating one of the members never came back to work after that day. Bitt planned old-school treatment for these guys if he ever located them. He envisioned taking them one by one on a medium-sized boat out into the ocean and hanging them upside down over the stern. A person hung in that way would experience hysteria, imbalance, and nausea. He also planned to have his tool box with him. It included just a few interesting items, such as long butane lighters; a hedge clipper; small, rusty saws; a pair of clean snippers; a pair of rusty snippers; straight razors; and box cutters. Bitt didn't plan to kill them but just intimidate them.

CHAPTER 11

Bitt's run of luck ended when Billy Carter again came to Florida and begged him to take him and his buyer to a big-time drug source. The Colombians and Cubans had met Carter before and weren't impressed with him. The former North Carolina basketball player usually dressed casually in sweat suits. Bitt, of course, was always dressed to the nines in designer clothes and expensive boots or shoes. That was more acceptable to the Latinos, who were as expensively dressed as they were dangerous. Carter's casual look offended the drug suppliers.

At about that time, many of the drug cartels took a hiatus. They periodically stopped their illegal businesses for two to three months to go home to Colombia or Cuba to be with their families and rest. This was a repeated pattern, and they informed Bitt when they were going to be on vacation. This happened during one of the times when Carter was pressing Bitt to help him and his friend make a buy. Bitt suspected that Carter was trying to supply meth pushers. Carter brought his own self-proclaimed trusted buyer, who turned out to be a DEA drug task force member. Carter and the imposter wanted to talk to Bitt about his supplier connections. Bitt was suspicious of Carter's request from day one. Bitt met with Carter and the agent a few times but exercised great care. He refused to acknowledge he even had connections, let alone who they were. He later learned that the agent was wired during these conversations.

A short time later, Carter, who didn't know his associate was with the DEA, managed to drag Bitt's friend Taylor Bishop into the fray. Still living in Atlanta, Carter contacted Bishop through a mutual friend and asked him to call Bitt. They were the closest of friends, and Bitt reluctantly agreed to introduce Carter and his new friend to the suppliers. By that time, his phone was bugged. One of his mistakes during several recorded calls was discussing an illegal bet he'd made, which would come back to haunt him. Carter was persistent about arranging a buy for the supposed dealer, and Bishop asked Bitt to work with the two, partially because a friend of Bishop in Atlanta was going to receive some of the soon-to-be-purchased cocaine from Carter. Bitt reluctantly agreed, and the ax soon fell. Carter had convinced Bishop that he was $10,000 short to make the buy from Bitt's connections. He told Bishop that if he would wire the funds to him or Bitt, he could make his buy, so everyone on both ends would be taken care of. Not trusting Carter, Bishop wired the $10,000 directly to Bitt via Western Union. Bitt had to go to three different Western Unions to get the entire $10,000, which seemed weird to him. Soon after he picked up the money, Bitt's world came crashing down.

The DEA videotaped Bitt picking up the money at all three locations. The true target of the sting operation was Jack Davidson. As it turned out, Davidson didn't get into any trouble, but Bitt and Carter did. The alleged agreement between Carter and the undercover agent was way too good to be true, but Bitt wasn't privy to the details, or he would have likely smelled a rat. The same day, prior to the cash pickups, a Pure Platinum employee borrowed Bitt's Corvette. Therefore, Bitt agreed to let Carter pick him up and take him to Western Union. They were being followed by unmarked cars and a DEA helicopter. The government agents considered it a bonus that Bitt and Carter went together to pick up the money being wired.

There were DEA agents posing as Western Union clerks at each location, and they directed Bitt and Carter to a second and third facility in order to receive the total amount of cash being wired. They told Bitt that there wasn't enough cash on hand at any one Western Union site to give him all of the money at once. Still feeling uneasy, Bitt refused to accompany Carter to deliver the money to make the drug purchase. Instead, Bitt asked to be dropped off at a Fort Lauderdale Denny's restaurant to get something to eat. He planned to call the Platinum colleague who'd borrowed his car to pick him up when he finished his meal. Fifteen minutes later, he was arrested, cuffed, and escorted out of the restaurant by DEA agents. Always a dapper dresser, he was wearing a tuxedo when he was transported to the Broward County Jail.

CHAPTER 12

Bitt spent about six months in jail. He expected no help from Davidson and didn't receive any. He was visited by several attorneys who wanted to represent him. They were mostly ambulance-chaser types. Soon a lawyer by the name of Jim Holmes visited and brought him his reading glasses. Bitt knew a friend had sent him, but he had no idea who. He suspected it was one of two girls he had been seeing, including Rosey Benson, who was living with him off and on by that time. Holmes was the guy in the legal field for representing criminal defendants in South Florida. He drove a Jaguar with a personalized plate: "WALK 'EM." Bitt had about $300,000 in get-away money in a safe-deposit box. He agreed to pay Holmes a fee of $100,000 upon being released. At the same time, one of Bitt's transplanted Georgia acquaintances, Scott Miller, was on the run from a deal gone sour in Atlanta and needed some cash. He borrowed Bitt's car from the Platinum employee who had used it the day Bitt was arrested. Miller, also known as Scott Alvarez, was involved in robbing the Platinum safe, which was unbelievably located outside in a shed instead of inside the club. Bitt believed that Miller had learned the safe's combination from watching him put cash in it. Miller stayed in the Fort Lauderdale area for several months, spending the stolen money and driving Bitt's Corvette.

Holmes didn't make contact with Bitt for six to eight weeks after the arrest, and Bitt quickly earned his way into the Thunder Dome at the jail. This area was reserved for the most unruly of the inmates, and Bitt quickly worked his way into the top-floor solitary accommodations. Within a week of his arrest, Bitt was removed from the general population after he beat up another prisoner in the TV room. The disagreement was over what TV program was going to be watched. He utilized the heel of one of his shoes, and it proved hard enough to make some dents in his opponent's face and head. From that incident forward, Bitt was only allowed to wear flat-soled tennis shoes. Never leaving his cell, Bitt was confused about his status when a DEA representative offered him a chance to earn his freedom. He was told that if he agreed to carry a box with five kilos of cocaine into the office of Jack Davidson, set it down, and announce, "Jack, here's your delivery," all charges against him would disappear, and he would be released. Bitt refused to cooperate, and he stayed in jail. He figured this desperate offer showed just how badly the DEA wanted Jack Davidson, a big-time player in the industry and owner of more than fifty clubs.

Bitt used his jail time as a chance to recuperate. He had abused his body for several years, and he started recovering by sleeping fourteen to sixteen hours a day. He made only one friend, who gave him some Twinkies before he was transferred to the Thunder Dome. He went from going outside one hour a week to being in his cell by himself twenty-four hours a day. Holmes negotiated Bitt's bond downward over a period of time. The Thrower family began to worry about Bitt when they couldn't reach him. They eventually learned from Rosey that he was incarcerated. She covered for him for a few weeks before admitting the truth. Rosey hung around a little while in Florida and then accepted a job as an exotic dancer in Hawaii. Bitt lost contact with her after she moved. However, a gentleman who lived with Rosey in Hawaii would later work for Bitt in the Atlanta club industry.

Bitt talked to his ex-wife, Cindy, and told her about his dilemma. His father used some farm property as collateral to help meet Bitt's bond requirement. The Thrower family knew Bitt was into illegal activities based on the many houses, cars, and other luxury items he purchased. Bitt's bail started out at $250,000, and Holmes worked on getting it reduced. Eventually, it was lowered to the point where the Throwers could raise enough funds by using land as collateral. When he was finally released, the first thing Bitt did was access his safety box and pay Holmes the $100,000 he owed him. Bitt did push-ups and sit-ups in jail, but mostly, he slept. He often had to be awakened for the roll call. He entered the jail with about $500 in his pocket, which was plenty to make weekly purchases from the commissary. Holmes liked the old-school method Bitt used to pay him, delivering the $100,000 in cash in a brown paper bag.

Leaving the Broward County Jail in the same tuxedo he'd been wearing when he was arrested, he was met by some drug boys upon his release. They took him somewhere to buy him some clothes, including underwear and socks. The Good Samaritans paid for a room for Bitt at the Oakland East Motor Lodge for a month. Before dropping him off at the room, they told him they were starved. They inquired if Bitt could get them ten that day, meaning ten kilos of cocaine. Bitt was shocked at the brashness of the request and replied that he hadn't had time to digest his meal yet, and he refused to cooperate. His response offended them, but Bitt told them he needed to ease back into the drug world and wasn't looking to have a Colombian necktie put around him if he waltzed in and asked for a deal less than twenty-four hours after being released.

Holmes cut a deal for Bitt to serve five years and figured that would amount to no more than six to eighteen months in prison. Bitt considered a sentence like that to be a cakewalk. Holmes apparently had a connection with a federal prosecutor who wanted to eventually work with him in private practice. It appeared that Bitt would get off as easily as could be expected. Then things went haywire. A major law enforcement sting led to the arrest of Holmes, formerly a judge; some DEA agents; some current judges; and several customs agents. A total of fifty to sixty arrests were made, and many deals, including the one arranged for Bitt, were considered tainted and invalid. Holmes reported to the authorities that Bitt had paid him only $20,000. The reality was that much of the $100,000 he'd given Holmes was used to grease the skids for the five-year deal about to be cut for Bitt. With those arrangements out the window, Bitt faced statutory federal penalties for his crimes, amounting to thirty years for trafficking and another thirty years for conspiracy. He was, unfortunately, back to square one.

Bitt was then assigned an attorney who worked pro bono for him since Bitt had already paid a fee. This new attorney represented Bitt for the next several years while the matter continued to bog down in a legal morass. There would never be a trial, and the matter wouldn't be settled till 2000. In the meantime, Bitt was effectively considered a felon. Cut loose on bail, he returned to the Atlanta area about one month following his release in late 1991. He found a job at a truck stop and nightclub, Southern Comfort, on Moreland Avenue. He was the manager and bouncer for $100 a night, and he could have all he wanted to eat. It was a redneck establishment with chicken wire in front of the stage to protect the performing bands. He kept the rough crowds under control, but he didn't forget he was released on a bail bond, and it was in his best interest to stay away from further trouble. Bitt performed bartending duties as well as bouncing and managing. He hired a few former associates and soon cleaned up the place in terms of making it safer to patronize. The inclination he'd had months earlier to get away from his lifestyle and return to his parents' home remained deeply buried in his heart. It would be quite some time before it made another appearance.

Soon Bitt found other employment. Bert Brewer, who owned the Fine Foxes, approached Bitt about working for him. He was the neighbor of Trill Jonesboro, the former owner of the Atlanta Falcons. Brewer fondly remembered Bitt bringing in a lot of people to the Foxes in the past and vastly improving the quality of the patrons and simultaneously boosting the club's revenues. Bitt had already called Sam Watterson at the Gold Club and asked for his job back. Watterson, now the Gold Club general manager, told Bitt he'd love to bring him back but couldn't get around the felony charges hanging over his head. Bitt was hired to work weekends at the Foxes and recruit employees during week nights. Brewer agreed to give Bitt $200 on the nights he wasn't working to try to talk dancers and employees of other clubs into coming to work for the Foxes.

Bitt did his best to make the club profitable and draw a higher class of customers. Within six months, he turned Foxes completely around, and it was making money hands over fists. However, it was wide open with drug usage, sex, and carousing. Bitt had a tough bunch of young kids who backed him up in the frequent confrontations to maintain order. Several WWE wrestlers frequented the Foxes, and Bitt fought more than one of them who refused to behave and leave on Bitt's demand. One wrestler in particular gave Bitt all he could handle, so he eventually hired him. Less than a year into his employment, Bitt became angry at Brewer. Bitt was relegated to the rear section of the club on New Year's Eve of 1991 by Brewer, who feared Bitt would admit too many people for free.

Immediately after New Year's Eve, Bitt's father had a serious heart attack and was hospitalized. The doctors thought he was going to die, but he hung in there. With all of that going on, Bitt quit his job at the Foxes. The family found Bitt's mother an apartment across the street from Crawford Long Hospital. Bitt took his stash with him, noticing that it was rapidly declining. Bitt began sitting with his father throughout the nights and reading to him, hoping he would be heard. One intern was impressed with Bitt's concern and encouraged him to not give up and to keep fighting for his father. Bitt was watching TV one night in the hospital and saw a story on a new nightclub opening in Sandy

Springs, Georgia, by the name of Norman's Tails. Bitt thought to himself that he might be lucky enough to find a job at the new spot.

He went to the club; met the owner, Frank Tardy; and handed him his résumé. Bitt was honest with Tardy about his legal troubles. Tardy was a former customer of the Gold Club and had met Bitt's buddy Sam Watterson. Tardy asked Watterson about Bitt, and he told him Bitt would get him girls and customers but would occasionally hammer people. With this glowing recommendation from Watterson, Bitt was hired as a bouncer. Bitt would leave his new club job and go straight to the hospital to sit with his father overnight. One morning, Bitt was reading to his unconscious father and holding his hand, when his father woke up. He said he felt as if he had been napping a short time and was amazed that he had been out for a few months. Unfortunately, Bitt's father was paralyzed from the neck down. Bitt was thrilled with his father's improvement, and his father was moved from ICU to a regular room. One morning a few days later, Bitt had an experience that briefly woke him up to realize that God was still working in his life. A lady from the Emory Rehabilitation Center came into the hospital room at eight o'clock on a Saturday morning. Bitt had already used the patient bathroom to clean up and get rid of the club smell. The attractive Emory employee looked at Bitt and said, "Bitt Thrower, how are you?" Bitt had no idea who she was; this was a common occurrence due to the number of people he met while working at the Gold Club.

The pretty Emory administrator asked Bitt how his father was doing. Bitt replied that he was doing pretty well for a guy who was not supposed to wake up again. She then told Bitt's father that she was going to have him picked up in a few hours to go to the Emory Rehabilitation Center for therapy. Bitt went with his father and quickly noticed that most of the other patients were much younger than his father, who was in his early seventies and more impaired than most of the other clients. On Monday morning, two days later, the Emory administrator asked Bitt a question. She wanted to know if he could tell her how she knew him and under what circumstances. Not giving Bitt time to answer, she told him that there was no one in the center like his father. She asked Bitt if he knew why he was admitted with such serious physical issues at such an advanced age, because she sure didn't. She further indicated that his father was barely alive, and she had no idea what had come over her to admit him to the center.

Bitt answered that he didn't know either, but later, he realized God's hand was involved in his father's unexplainable admission for care. To everyone's surprise, his father made great progress. Within a month, he was wrestling on his knees with his therapist. In another month, he was home and functioning at a higher level than thought possible. He was far from his physical stature before his heart attack, but Bitt was thrilled with the extent to which he improved. Bitt's mother even had to hide her husband's truck keys to keep him from taking off so much.

CHAPTER 13

Bitt was happy to be working at Norman's Tails, which changed its name to Stormin' Norman's only a few weeks later. He had no idea he would remain employed by the owners of that club and sister clubs for the next twenty years. He also became involved in more side jobs over time. Bitt soon learned that the other owner of the club was Bob Ireland, who would turn out to be his boss, friend, mentor, and major supporter. Ireland owned a string of lingerie shops and got into the strip club business by lending financial support to Frank Tardy's struggling joint to prevent impending bankruptcy. The deal was made quickly with the assistance of the highly intelligent Steve Youngleson, the premier adult entertainment attorney in the Southeast at that time. Youngleson avoided a soon-to-occur state bankruptcy action involving Norman's by filing for bankruptcy in federal court.

Youngleson knew that federal bankruptcy court superseded state bankruptcy court, and the matter was released to the federal court, buying time for Tardy and Ireland to work out their co-ownership details for Stormin' Norman's.

With his financial troubles solved, Tardy hired family members, his girlfriend, and some close friends to run the club with Bitt. Changing overnight from a steak restaurant to a strip club, Stormin' Norman's received a lot of local publicity and quickly became a hot spot. Bitt was responsible for much of the club's immediate success, as his friends, including the dope boys with whom he continued to maintain relationships, came in droves. It was a wide-open environment, and the patrons wanted it that way. Tardy also hired two guys who were fired from the Gold Club, even though they were lazy by Bitt's standards. He was hustling all over town and handing out business cards with promises of free cover charges or free drinks at Norman's.

At the time, Bitt didn't know Ireland from the man in the moon. However, he did know an older gentleman who came in most nights with two black bodyguards. Bitt always greeted him as he did other customers and seated him in a corner, per his request. One night, the regular customer asked Bitt to join him briefly at his table. He asked Bitt if he knew who he was, and Bitt replied, "No, sir." Ireland's bodyguards were Ricky Bishop and Sylvester Jackson, and like their boss, they were dressed in upscale clothing. They made Bitt feel a little uncomfortable, but they never caused any trouble, and they kept everyone away from Ireland. During this initial conversation between them, Ireland told Bitt he was the co-owner of the club. He then asked him to come to his office tomorrow and handed him a business card. Bitt agreed to come see him first thing in the morning. Bitt arrived on time and then waited three hours for Ireland to show up. Bitt would find Ireland's lack of punctuality to be a common occurrence in the years to follow.

Ireland informed Bitt that Tardy thought he was stealing from the club because people were always giving him money. He then asked Bitt if he was selling drugs in the club. Bitt assured him that was not the case and explained that he made a lot of tips due to his work ethic. He noted that he tried to give the customers the tables they wanted and sent over the girls they were interested in meeting. He shared that he didn't sit around but hustled all of the time, both inside and outside of the club. Bitt assured Ireland that he wasn't taking any cover money and pointed out, "There's

From Nightlife to Eternal Life

a door guy who collects these charges." Ireland then asked Bitt why the girls gave him money, and he replied that he took care of the girls by carrying their bags, escorting them to and from their running cars, and sending customers to them who would tip for their attentions. He explained that it was customary in the girlie business for internal tipping to occur between workers who assisted each other to get the most money possible out of the patrons. He added that this was a practice customarily followed in most nightclubs.

Ireland then asked Bitt, "What's going on at the club?"

This reminded him of the time he'd heard that same question from Jack Davidson. Bitt responded, "Do you want me to tell you what you want to hear, or do you want the truth?" Ireland said to tell him the truth, and Bitt did just that. He began by saying that the doorman was pocketing enough of the cover charges that he was likely making $1,000 a night in extra money. He reported that the doorman had a relationship with the pawnshop owner a couple of doors down and showed up every day in new clothes. He added that the doorman also bought gold and silver from the pawnshop owner's son, who stole it from his dad. He had no idea that Ireland was close to the doorman and had made sure he was hired by Tardy. Ireland expressed doubt that the doorman would steal from him, because they'd served together in Vietnam. Bitt told him he had a right to his opinion.

Bitt then continued that the bartenders, Tardy's girlfriend, and his wife were putting the receipts from about every third drink sold in their tip jar. Ireland wanted to know if Tardy was involved, and Bitt said probably not because he was lazy and never came out of his office. Bitt said he was caked up with cocaine every night and only came out to gulp down four to five drinks. He added that he occasionally had a girl come into his office for his personal entertainment as well. Bitt then told Ireland that he estimated Ireland was losing as much as 30 to 35 percent of the receipts to thievery. Ireland believed part of what Bitt told him but not all of it. He came up with a plan to see if Bitt was right. He gave Bitt a clicker so he could stand close to the door and count the number of people entering the club. Unbeknownst to Bitt, Ireland had another of his employees from another business in the parking lot doing the same thing. Bitt soon learned that he and the outside counter were never more than ten off of each other's numbers for a two-week period. The usual number of customers entering during the test was 150 to 220. Only 100 to 150 cover charges were being turned in to management.

Ireland then told Bitt he knew he couldn't be stealing despite Tardy's accusations, and Bitt heartily agreed with him. Ireland fired the doorman and put one of his bodyguards, Ricky Bishop, on the door. Bishop was a hulk of a man with a polite disposition unless he was provoked. He was the son of a female preacher and was destined to serve time in federal prison before succumbing to diabetes. Ireland also followed Bitt's recommendation and hired his own bartenders. In the new system, Bitt never touched the money, and he told Ireland, "As long as people walk through the doors and there are girls dancing, I'm going to make my money." Bitt was now making $500 a week in salary and pulling in about $1,500 in tips. Ireland and Tardy got into a disagreement over Ireland's personnel changes. In time, Ireland bought out Tardy for $400,000. Bitt had a new boss who respected him.

Bitt was now sharing an apartment with Janice Banta, who was soon to be the mother of his son. Banta was a beautiful Hispanic American who played college basketball at Mississippi State University. She and Bitt were not only lovers but also buddies. They worked out and rode horses together. She was to become Bitt's second wife before long. Before selling his interest to Ireland, Tardy reached out to mobster Carlo Marcello's son, Angelo, who was an outcast, considered untrustworthy, and not a made man. Trouble soon began. The Marcellos operated in New Orleans and were out of their territory in Atlanta, which was considered Gambino family territory. One morning, Bishop, the new doorman, called Bitt and asked him if he had been fired by Ireland. Bitt said he didn't know and met Bishop at the club. Neither Bishop's key nor Bitt's key unlocked the club entrance. Bitt called Ireland at his mansion in the Sandy Springs area. Ireland had no idea what was going on, and he came to the club and found that his master key also didn't fit. It turned out to be a move by Marcello's son to intimidate Ireland and his crew. Tardy and the younger Marcello had changed out all of the locks at Stormin' Norman's. Ireland called a locksmith he often used. The locksmith told him he'd had an emergency call to change all of the locks at the club at six o'clock that morning. It was an attempt to force the club to pay the young Marcello and his cronies for protection.

On the following Sunday night, Bitt and Sylvester Jackson, the other Ireland bodyguard and a club employee, were inventorying the onsite liquor stock, when the phone rang. It was Angelo Marcello, and he asked to speak with Ireland. He had already squeezed a couple of other small Atlanta clubs into signing agreements with him, and now he wanted into Stormin' Norman's. Since his lock-changing event backfired, he told Ireland that he was coming over to kill him unless he immediately cooperated with him and let him buy his way into the club. Ireland refused. After the count was finished, Bitt, Ireland, and Jackson were sitting on the front-porch area of the club, relaxing and discussing what they were going to do. As always, Ireland and Jackson were armed. Lo and behold, thirty minutes after the threatening call was received, a car pulled up to the front of the club. It was a big Cadillac. They recognized Angelo Marcello in the driver's seat. Bitt jumped up and dragged Marcello out of the car through the window. He then beat the hoodlum up, leaving him temporarily incapacitated. In the meantime, Jackson grabbed the other occupant of the car and held him at gunpoint. Bitt disarmed Marcello's colleague and then administered a serious beating to him with his own gun.

Two days later, a one-time Gambino associate, Cale Snelling, took a call informing him that the Marcellos had put out a contract on Bitt. Snelling was a disbarred Jewish attorney who'd previously worked for the Gambinos but parted with them on good terms when he lost his license. Ireland had hired him to do his legal work, understanding that he couldn't appear in court or put his name on most legal documents. However, Snelling knew the law and was gifted in handling business affairs for Ireland. Bitt learned of this threat and was also told that a couple of Gambino heavies would come to the club to protect Bitt. They did so for the next two weeks, and nothing happened. Though he rarely did so, Bitt carried a gun during that time. A few weeks later, an evening meeting at Stormin' Norman's was requested and set up between representatives of the Marcello family and the Gambino family to discuss the conflict. Bitt set up an arrangement of long tables and closed the club shortly before an array of large limousines pulled into the parking lot. There were as many bodyguards as meeting participants involved, a total of about twelve. The old man himself, Carlo Marcello, was present. The decision was made to banish Angelo from Atlanta, a city clearly flagged as belonging to the Gambinos.

The small-statured Carlo Marcello asked to speak with Bitt after the meeting. Bitt agreed to speak with him but was understandably nervous. The diminutive elder Marcello, who used a cane, told him that his son had acted outside his level of authority. In a humble, polite manner, he apologized for Angelo's actions. He advised that he understood his son had pulled a gun on Bitt, but the ensuing beating he'd received may have gone a little too far. Nevertheless, Marcello told Bitt that he owed him a favor for not doing further harm to his son. He told Bitt, "If you ever need anything in the city of New Orleans, you come to me, and it's done." Bitt never took him up on the offer and never saw him again.

CHAPTER 14

From that point forward, Bitt and Ireland became thick as thieves and developed a strong friendship. At that point in the early 1990s, Bitt had no feelings of guilt or concern about his spirituality. He remained in some contact with his family but didn't make it to see them as often as he would have liked. He frequently didn't see them at Christmas or on other holidays. They loved Bitt despite knowing he was up to no good. He began a long period of employment at Stormin' Norman's as the general manager. He excelled at running things in the club and keeping the customers happy while raking in good tips night in and night out. Bitt was living with Banta at the time. He first met her when she worked as a waitress at the Gold Club. Bitt was attracted to her stunning good looks, and they enjoyed each other's company at first. He and Banta eventually had a son. She left him five years later after a contentious divorce finalized in 2000.

Tardy was out of the picture after selling out his interest in Stormin' Norman's to Ireland. Bitt settled into a six-day workweek—on nights, of course. Ireland didn't believe in vacations. Prior to Tardy being bought out, Ireland made sure Bitt was in his camp. One night at the club, he asked Bitt to state which team he was on. Bitt confirmed he was strongly behind Ireland. That was a good thing for Bitt, as Tardy had fired him on several occasions over a few months, and Ireland had always rehired him. Tardy had continued to claim Bitt was stealing money, which was untrue. Tardy's judgment was undoubtedly affected by his heavy drinking and chronic use of cocaine. After he lost ownership, Tardy came into the club one night and screamed at Ireland that he had taken advantage of him in the buyout he'd previously agreed to accept. Sylvester Jackson cold-cocked Tardy and knocked him out. Tardy never set foot in the club again.

During the next few months, Bitt stayed in touch with a friend who worked as head of security for the Fine Foxes Club, Bodie Perez. A colorful character, Perez was formerly a DEA task force member and also had put in time with the Henry County Sherriff's

Department. Perez introduced Bitt to Douglas Donlan, a Georgia Bureau of Investigation (GBI) agent. He would become tight with Bitt in the future. Donlan told Bitt he needed to get ahead of the legal issues still hanging over his head. Donlan wanted to know what Bitt was willing to do or talk about in order to receive some assistance with his pending Florida charges. Local law enforcement wanted to take Ireland down, but Bitt never turned on his good friend and mentor. Ireland had drawn the ire of the local police and sheriff because he had used a legal loophole to open the club in Sandy Springs, an exclusive Atlanta suburb. His longtime attorney, Steve Youngleson, paved the legal way for Stormin' Norman's to remain in business. There was clearly no other establishment like this club in or around trendy upper-class Sandy Springs.

Bitt was kidnapped twice by different law enforcement teams. The first group consisted of members of the Fulton County Police Department and the FBI. After inviting him into a car, they drove around and tried to reason with him. They offered Bitt their assistance in making his legal troubles go away if he helped them nail Ireland. They told Bitt that Ireland was connected to organized crime. They said they would take anything he could give them to get to Ireland. The truth didn't seem to be a big factor in their request. Bitt listened to their proposal but refused. He had been treated well by Ireland. He knew Ireland's only connection to the Gambinos was through Cale Snelling, the disbarred attorney. The police and the FBI warned Bitt not to let Ireland know they had approached him. He immediately told Ireland what had transpired, and they both reached the conclusion that the authorities were hoping to close the club down. Donlan was to be disappointed in Bitt, because he wanted to cultivate him as a source of information.

A few months later, word again reached Bitt that his likely sentence in Florida for trafficking and conspiracy would be sixty years. That got his attention. In order to increase his chances of avoiding jail, Bitt gave Donlan a few tips regarding drug deals he learned of while working in the club. A club customer calling himself George Uboa became a regular at the club and befriended Bitt. Uboa lived in the Country Club of the South, an exclusive neighborhood with estate-style properties. Bitt had visited his house a couple of times. The property included a pool built on the edge of a precipice, with built-in neon lighting in the walls. Uboa flashed a lot of money around and let Bitt know he was involved in heroin sales and credit card scams. Uboa loved being with beautiful women, and Bitt made sure he was always taken care of in that area when he visited the club. Bitt gave Donlan Uboa's name and license tag number. He had no idea that the DEA had been after Uboa for the past five years for credit card theft as well as heroin distribution.

Bitt gave Donlan the information on a Thursday night. Donlan quickly researched the law enforcement databases. This activity set off a flurry of red flags. Two days later, on Saturday morning, Bitt answered the door because someone was pounding on it. Standing in the entryway were representatives from the DEA, the Secret Service, the CIA, and the FBI. Mark Hanigan of the DEA, who later accepted a senior DEA posting in South America, led a contingent of agents into Bitt's home. They asked Bitt to accompany them for a ride. He had only been asleep for a couple of hours but agreed to go with them. He accepted with the idea in mind that he might earn some help with his legal problems. They rode around in a black van and parked at an out-of-the-way spot. He was grilled by Hanigan, who told him he was guilty of a litany of felony charges. Bitt stood up to him and told them they weren't going to scare him and run roughshod over him. Actually, he was terrified. He listened to the agents and was overwhelmed that he was at the center of their attention. He quickly found out that these agents were hungry to arrest Uboa. They had come close to catching Uboa, but he kept slipping through their grasp.

Bitt was suspicious of whether they would truly make his charges go away and told them he would think about their request to turn informer. Bitt told Ireland about the offer. Ireland was in favor of the arrangement because he felt it would afford protection for his club from the local authorities. Donlan called Bitt again on Monday and told him he had been told of the offer, and he encouraged Bitt to accept it. An unsuspecting Uboa discussed getting into the club and girlie business with Bitt. One Saturday morning a few weeks later, Uboa came to the club and showed Bitt a box with $700,000 in it. He was by himself, and he wanted to show Bitt that he could come up with cash quickly in order to buy Stormin' Norman's or another local club. Bitt was wide-eyed while staring at that much money and would have robbed him and disposed of him, but he was pretty sure Uboa was under surveillance. This fact saved Uboa's life. Uboa came into the club every night to see pretty girls and talk with Bitt. He was flashy and normally came in alone. He occasionally bragged about being a prince in Nigeria.

Bitt talked about many things with Uboa, including drugs and nightclubs. Uboa continued to invite Bitt to go in with him and run whatever club he ended up buying. Bitt took his time in setting up Uboa for a fall. He fed information to Donlan, who shared it with the other agencies. They wanted Bitt to learn about the drug trade, credit card fraud, and money-laundering activities. They were impatient in their demands, which were passed on through Donlan. Bitt landed another invitation to Uboa's lavish home and passed the word on. The day of the visit, he was fitted with a Nagra listening device. At that time, the devices were huge and had to be taped in the small of his back with an elastic band. Bitt felt as if he had a phone book taped to him. He wore the recorder, outfitted with tape reels, and went to Uboa's house. He feared that his ruse would be exposed if he asked too many questions. Uboa was drinking heavily and became loose-tongued. He told Bitt about the breakdown of his criminal enterprises, including drug distribution and credit card theft. Bitt thought he had secured plenty for the government to build its case. However, the assistant who'd placed the Nagra on Bitt forgot to turn it on. Bitt was livid. He couldn't believe a simple omission had ruined the effort he had gone to in getting Uboa to talk so freely.

Donlan asked Bitt to try it again in a week, and Bitt told him he was crazy. He convinced Donlan that he would have to bide his time until another good opportunity arose. Bitt was eventually invited back to Uboa's house, and again, he went in wired. This time, the recorder was running, but Uboa didn't give Bitt as much information as he had the first time. The primary topic of conversation was drugs, and Uboa told Bitt he used the services of Albanian pilots to fly cocaine from South America to the United States. A short time later, Bitt approached Uboa and told him he wasn't making enough money at the club and wanted to score a big sale of heroin. He convinced Uboa that Ireland was bankrolling the deal and said he wanted to buy five kilos of heroin from him. Uboa helped him by introducing him to the Albanian pilot who secured heroin and cocaine for him from Colombia and flew it to the States. Bitt convinced Uboa that he would make a nice commission, and he planned to move the drugs by selling them at Stormin' Norman's and other clubs employing many of his friends and acquaintances. Uboa bit hook, line, and sinker.

The pilot continued to frequent the club, and he eventually brought Bitt a sample of cocaine. He tested it out at 94 percent purity, which was confirmed by the DEA. Everyone agreed it was the real deal, nearly uncut product. Uboa had more than a hundred people involved in Atlanta, in New York, and on the West Coast. Postal employees were intercepting credit cards that were in the mail and intended for appropriate recipients. Bitt took about a month to put the pilot at ease; he knew better than to rush him. He built up a rapport with the pilot and started hinting at making a buy. He had experience in that area from his time in Florida, and he knew he couldn't push things too fast. Uboa had already informed the pilot that Bitt was interested in buying product. The pilot told Bitt he owned his plane and made frequent trips to Colombia. Bitt continued to make the pilot feel special by giving him free drinks and sending girls his way. After a couple of months, Bitt approached him and told him he wanted to get back into the drug business. One night, the pilot brought an ounce of cocaine and indicated he was ready to make a deal. Bitt performed a self-test on the cocaine and verified how good it was.

On the day the deal was to go down, Bitt flashed some money to the pilot. He showed him $30,000 to pay for a kilo and told him he had the rest of the money for the remaining four kilos. The pilot was to pick up the drugs from someone else in the area and was under the impression that Ireland was providing the funds. Of course, it was actually the DEA who supplied the cash to corral Uboa. There were close to thirty DEA agents in place for the takedown inside and outside the club. Bitt initially felt guilty for his role, but over time, he became immune to those feelings. One DEA agent in particular irritated Bitt. At a meeting shortly before the string of arrests were kicked off, he rubbed Bitt the wrong way. The meeting was to allow the different agencies to cooperate and arrange for a series of arrests across the country in connection with the credit card fraud. The agent who disliked Bitt was criticizing him and telling him he was going to blow it. In front of his colleagues, Bitt challenged him to a fight if he would take off his badge. Bitt informed him that he beat up people tougher than him every day using only his left hand. Bitt had slept only a few hours for the last three nights, which made him more prone to lose his temper. Bitt later learned that the agent giving him a hard time had been trying to make a case against Uboa for five years and had never come close to the point Bitt had reached.

Bitt flashed $150,000 to encourage the pilot to get the drugs and bring them back to the parking lot of the Kroger in midtown Atlanta. The DEA went so far as to secure a car that looked like the one owned by Ireland to deliver the money to the parking lot so Bitt could supposedly seal the deal. Bitt agreed to let the pilot leave with $30,000 if he agreed to quickly bring back one kilo so he could confirm the quality in advance of parting with the remaining $120,000 for the rest of the buy. The pilot left, and interestingly, the DEA lost him. Therefore, the down payment was in the wind. More importantly, the location of the drug stash house was not determined. When the pilot returned about an hour later with the cocaine, he was arrested. Simultaneously, about a hundred other people were rounded up across the country, which ended their involvement with the credit card fraud and the drug trade being perpetrated by Uboa. This represented the first of many takedowns Bitt would participate in as an informant and undercover person. He was also pseudo-arrested for appearance's sake, but the cuffs were removed as soon as the pilot was taken away to jail. Uboa and the pilot were eventually extradited to their home countries of Nigeria and Albania to face unknown and likely unpleasant consequences.

CHAPTER 15

Bitt's next involvement with the DEA came to be known as the Gold Rush. Tony Pepp, the Gambino capo in Atlanta, met Bitt and became a good friend over time. The Gambinos wanted to get into the nightclub business and explored the possibility of cutting a deal with Ireland to nudge their way into Stormin' Norman's, which had become extremely successful. Ireland's string of lingerie shops provided the financial backing for the club. Bitt organized a surprise birthday party for Ireland in the club and invited 150 of his friends. He talked him into coming into the club by telling him he'd had to kill Angelo Marcello because he had come busting into the club. Bitt said he'd double-tapped Marcello and needed help getting rid of the body. Ireland said he'd be right over and to wait for him. Bitt realized after that conversation that he had a true partner, one who would drop everything and show up immediately to help him cover up a murder. That was the type of loyalty Bitt appreciated and willingly reciprocated. The surprise party was a huge success, but the demonstration of camaraderie from Ireland touched Bitt's heart.

Ireland never agreed to do business with the Gambinos but enjoyed a friendly relationship with them. The Gambinos were receiving inside information about a federal prisoner in the Atlanta penitentiary, an incarcerated major drug dealer from Tennessee. A snitch told the Gambinos that this drug kingpin had buried a huge amount of cash on his extensive land holdings in Tennessee, supposedly hundreds of millions of dollars. The informant was also, unbeknownst to the Gambino family, talking to the DEA in the hopes of securing a reduced sentence. Meanwhile, the DEA searched thousands of acres of the prisoner's Tennessee property to no avail.

Duke Flagler, a well-known gun for hire, worked at various times for crime syndicates and the government—whoever was willing to pay him. He had also worked on a few drug deals with Bitt involving high-quality cocaine from Peru. Working in the early '90s for the Gambinos, Flagler put together a team to find the hidden Tennessee treasure. Several men hired by Flagler were placed in a rental house onsite next to the prisoner's land to be ready to dig when a good lead was secured for the location of the stash. Elaborate plans were in place to secure the area, including incapacitating but not harming the locals, to allow for a successful extraction. The DEA and the Gambinos had no idea they were both looking for the money. Before coming clean on the exact location of the money, the drug dealer died in prison from natural causes. He never told anyone where his cash was buried, and to Bitt's knowledge, it was never found. Flagler later began working for organized crime interests in Chicago to oversee their Las Vegas operations.

Joe Castellano, a soldier with the New York Gambino family, met Bitt during management meetings that took place on the back deck of Stormin' Norman's. Bitt was recruited to be part of the crew that would drop everything immediately and go to Tennessee when the location of the money was determined. He was promised a $2 million payday for his assistance. The Gambino onsite team had amassed a cache of weapons and extraction equipment ready to use when needed. Flagler organized the meetings, which included a small group of veterans with whom he had served in Vietnam. He referred to them as the Legends. Bitt told Ireland about his involvement with the Gambino team concerning the Gold Rush. Although the project never came to fruition, Bitt's stature as a valid informant and one attached to organized criminal activities was enhanced in the DEA's eyes. Bitt's reputation as a connected criminal with involvement in drug dealing and other illegal activities grew larger than life. He was given credit for many crimes he had nothing to do with.

Bitt still catered to celebrities at Stormin' Norman's but not to the extent he had at the Gold Club. He saw a darker element in that more drug dealers and suppliers frequented Norman's, and he knew most of them on a first-name basis. The GBI, specifically Donlan, kept Bitt active as an informant over the next several years. Soon the Greek mob made an appearance on the north side of Atlanta in the person of Theo Lombopolus. As owner of the first club in trendy Sandy Springs, Ireland offered him free legal services from Attorney Youngleson to write legal legislation to ban other clubs from doing business locally. Lombopolus opened a club, the Raven, and convinced Ireland to become a co-owner. This agreement allowed the new club to meet the local requirements to be in business. Lombopolus and Ireland opened up six or seven more clubs around Atlanta but didn't sink the appropriate resources into them. They weren't managed by Bitt but by John Trill, who had experience in running clubs in New York and Atlanta. He convinced Ireland and Lombopolus he could run their string of clubs but had no connection with Stormin' Norman's.

Ireland put a different touch in practice at the Raven: nude male dancers. However, Trill couldn't make the clubs placed under his control work, and they all closed down inside of a year. Little did Ireland realize at the time that he had the best club organizer and manager in Atlanta in the form of Bitt Thrower. He had an inkling of the truth after the new clubs failed, and he made Bitt the general manager of Norman's, giving him a raise. Bitt didn't care much about the raise since he was making $2,500 a week in tips. He would hold on to his pay checks till he had enough to buy something he wanted to acquire, such as new clothes or gifts for a girlfriend. Ireland also told Bitt he was ready to remodel Norman's, which still looked like a barbecue restaurant. Bitt thought Ireland had finally seen the light. He asked Bitt to personally handle the remodeling and gave him a check for $800. Bitt was amazed at his lack of understanding of renovation costs, since $800 might buy one couch. Ireland, on the other hand, thought he had given Bitt a lot of money.

Bitt was wondering how he could do anything with $800, when a fax came across his office desk. He read a public invitation to a going-out-of-business liquidation sale by Eastern Airlines. It was the early '90s, and he was one of the few individuals who showed up to what was effectively an auction. He bought 150 nice cushioned chairs for two dollars apiece and fifty tables for four dollars each. He then called in a favor from a friend to provide new carpet for the club. His acquaintance was the son of a carpet dealer, and he gave Bitt carpet, free delivery, and free installation. Bitt used the remaining money to buy paint, and the staff held a weekend painting party. Effectively, Ireland got his club remodeled for $800. Bitt's successful remodeling project convinced Ireland to turn him loose. Bitt talked Ireland into building a large stage and putting in huge mirrors. Bitt called in favors to bring down much of the cost of the new stage, and he installed neon lighting with his own money. He also upgraded the dancers at Norman's and mixed them in with Ireland's lingerie girls, freeing some to return to their modeling activities.

At the time, Amos Blatt and Ross Angle became interested

in the club. Both were well-known local bookies dubbed as the "country club bookies." They expressed an interest in getting into the girlie business and enlisted Bitt's help in finding a club to purchase. They were impressed with Norman's success and wanted to buy it, but Ireland asked for $3.5 million. Bitt found a downtown joint for Blatt and Angle, the Centerfold. He negotiated a purchase for $200,000. Blatt and Angle were now club owners. Unfortunately, Angle had a cocaine habit. Bitt was offered a job at the Centerfold as well as part ownership. He told Ireland he was leaving to make the newly purchased club profitable. It was his first venture into club ownership, but it would be a brief one. Bitt spent about three weeks there after sprucing it up. Several of the staff from Norman's came with Bitt.

A ring was installed near the stage for bachelor parties. Bitt borrowed from his Florida nightlife experiences and arranged for soon-to-be-married men or customers looking for a fun time to strip down and wear oversized boxers. They were placed in the ring while nude dancers wrestled them and cleaned them with sponges. Most of the participants tried, often in vain, to keep their boxers in place. The club prospered and began bringing in $30,000 a week in just a few months. However, Angle caused problems by pawing the girls and trash-talking customers, all the while with his collectors and bodyguards nearby. One night, Bitt had all he could take of Angle's belligerence and told him he was a nuisance. He advised him to take his drug-addled behavior to someone else's establishment so it didn't hurt business at their club. Angle didn't take his invitation well and told Bitt exactly what he thought of his suggestion. Bitt knew he couldn't keep the club successful if one of the owners was continually out of line with the employees and customers, so he tuned him up. He slammed Angle on the bar, and some of his teeth were loosened. Angle was cut before his two accomplices dragged him outside. The bartender kept a shotgun behind the bar, and Angle's guys knew he was willing and able to use it.

The barkeep had killed a patron at the Centerfold a few weeks earlier. Bitt received a call while at Turner Field, where he was attending an Atlanta Braves 1992 play-off game. It was the bartender, who told Bitt he needed him to come in immediately because he had killed someone. He explained that he had left the door unlocked, and someone came into the club before it was open. When told the establishment was closed, the man refused to leave. A struggle ensued, and the bartender knocked the intruder down a flight of stairs, killing him. He told Bitt over the phone that not knowing what to do, he had placed the body in a Dumpster. Bitt told him to get the body out of the Dumpster, clean it up, and put it back where it had been. The police were not that interested, as the deceased had drugs in his blood and was a known vagabond. A surviving family member threatened to sue the club but settled for a $100,000 payment in exchange for dropping the matter.

Soon after tuning up Angle, Bitt was called by Amos Blatt, who informed him that the three-man ownership arrangement wasn't going to work out. Bitt's only investment had been sweat equity, and he agreed to take $70,000 to go away. Bitt immediately called the old man, Bob Ireland, and went to meet him at Norman's. He was rehired and began working the next night. The current night manager was reassigned to the day shift for Bitt to resume the nighttime management. One of Ireland's good friends, Jacob Foxe, was also an Atlanta club owner and knew Bitt from his friendship with Ireland and his patronage of Stagger Lee's. Foxe was not a chummy friend of Bitt's but would influence him in the years to come, although not in a good way. Foxe blew up a competing nightclub directly across the street from his place and wound up serving time in a federal prison. Unfortunately, a similar experience awaited Bitt down the road.

CHAPTER 16

Bitt returned to work at Norman's, and its popularity and profitability grew. By the end of 1992, he was again running the club and making good money. However, the feds continued to stay in touch with Bitt. He fed them information to make some drug busts and takedowns. Bitt and his wife, the former Janice Banta, were married and living on a horse farm in Braselton, Georgia. Banta, who was pregnant, was working at the Gold Club, which didn't bother Bitt, as she made good money. He allowed some bad guys from Jamaica to bring up truckloads of marijuana and store it in his barn, but he told the GBI about the arrangement so they could bust them. In the meantime, Bitt had negotiated a bonus plan with Ireland and Lombopolus to receive $50,000 in early 1993. He needed the money to pay a balloon payment due on his mortgage. He had used most of his buyout money from

From Nightlife to Eternal Life

the Centerfold to make a down payment on the farm. Bitt didn't know it at the time, but Ireland would not come through on the promised bonus, causing him to lose the property.

Bitt was always hustling on the side for deals big and small. He arranged for Ireland to buy fifty cashmere sweaters from a Macy's employee stealing from his employer. Ireland paid $1.50 apiece for the sweaters. The payoff for these arrangements was that the perpetrator would be someone special in the club. Bitt also became involved in boosting new cars from dealer lots in the wee hours of the morning. This led the authorities to question him vigorously to no avail. At the time, Bitt was a friend of the country singer Travis Tritt. However, after he was questioned by the police more than once about Bitt's car-stealing activities, Tritt broke off all contact. A friend of the club, Tritt began patronizing other nightclubs instead. This hurt Bitt, as he had done favors for Tritt, including organizing a signing party at the Gold Club. While he was a regular at Stormin' Norman's, Tritt even asked Bitt for his opinion of a new song he had recorded. Bitt asked him about the background noise he heard over the singing, and Tritt responded that it was the sound of running water because he had made the demo while taking a shower. There were still plenty of celebrities at

Norman's, including several Atlanta Braves. It was the best of the North Atlanta clubs and drew customers who had money to burn.

One criminal, who went by Little John, was a well-known meth cooker who had narrowly avoided being indicted on drug-related charges in New York City. He cooked for any customer, including organized crime and international drug distributors. A lot of pot was making its way into the United States from Jamaica. The CIA told Bitt to work Little John, whom he had met at Norman's. They were interested in the routes that the pot traveled to make it to America. Bitt worked his way into meeting with the Jamaicans by stating he wanted to buy a thousand pounds of pot. He later sold guns to them. Little John agreed to introduce him to the main men, and they flew to Miami to meet with the pot crew. Reacting to pressure from the feds, Bitt offered Ireland's money to buy the pot from the drug gang. He sold guns supplied by the CIA in the form of AK-47s. The Jamaicans were in a tough position because they had committed to delivering a load of pot, but the truck carrying it was hijacked.

Bitt refused to wear a wire and walked into a small ghetto house populated by several tough-looking Rastafarians. He sat on the floor as instructed, and soon ten to twelve Jamaicans stood behind him and dry-fired their guns—*click, click, click*. Bitt turned around, stared in their faces, and asked, "Are you guys having a good time? If you want to shoot me, put one in the chamber, and drill me. But if you want to do business, let's get down to it. If you don't like me, I'm out of here." One of the Jamaicans was suspicious of Bitt and made it clear he wasn't happy, but Bitt eventually made a deal and traded twenty AK-47s for pot, giving the drug crew the option of keeping the guns or selling them for cash. The drug crew wanted guns over cash. The CIA eventually got what they wanted in terms of the shipping routes, as Bitt went to South America himself and observed the transportation of pot, including identifying the employees working in customs who looked the other way when necessary. The feds always took the delivered pot, making sure Bitt didn't have access to it. He reported on all he learned during his initial visit to his contact, Donlan. Things went so well that Bitt made two more trips and sold more guns, specifically AK-47s, each time. Donlan rode on the back of Bitt's information to rise in the ranks of the GBI from field agent to superhero. Bitt even took some cocaine buyers to Rome, Georgia, for an alleged buy so Donlan could make an arrest in his hometown.

During the decade of the 1990s, Bitt continually made purchases, mostly of cocaine, ten kilos here and fifteen kilos there, so the CIA could gain information with respect to the principals involved and the methods of delivery. Ireland knew Bitt was doing odd jobs and gladly put up with him being absent for a day or two once a month or so. He felt that this arrangement made his club more secure and would stave off any legal efforts by the local government to pull his license or close the club. Bitt still was full of himself at that point in his life and had no concern for his spiritual well-being. There was too much money and excitement to pursue. He made several overseas trips in the early '90s for government agencies. He was sent on assignments to the likes of Colombia, Guatemala, and Costa Rica. Bitt came to learn that Uncle Sam had no qualms about whom he used to get what he wanted. He was continually surprised at how little regard the US government had for the addictive danger of the drugs. The contraband was typically confiscated for use in future agency sting operations and, at times, was put back in circulation for the purpose of catching more bad guys. It was clear to Bitt that some US drug abusers were using narcotic products that had passed through the hands of their own government.

CHAPTER 17

In November 1992, Bitt left the employ of Bob Ireland a second time. This event was triggered by the $50,000 bonus he was promised and never received. Fortunately, Bitt met Boris Jonesboro at Norman's. Jonesboro, a black man, was a retired colonel in the military and owned several nightclubs in Augusta, Georgia, that catered primarily to black men. He was well known and appeared in a few issues of *Jet Magazine*, which recognized him as a successful black entrepreneur. Prior to being stiffed regarding his bonus, Bitt brokered a deal to secure another nightclub for Jonesboro in Augusta and was awarded 20 percent ownership for his efforts. He was now an equal partner in this venture with Ireland, Lombopolus, Jonesboro, and James Lewis, an Atlanta resident who would serve time for tax evasion in the future. It was called the Speak Easy but later became Dolls Downtown. Bitt ran a van from Norman's to Augusta a few times a week, transporting dancers and checking on the club's operations. It was his first experience with a black nightclub. It was being managed by Bodie Perez, the former DEA task force agent who had also worked at the Fine Foxes in Atlanta.

Bitt found that his new club was a dog, only bringing in about $10,000 to $12,000 per week. However, he saw a lot of potential, especially because the competing white clubs were not well run. Bitt went to them and observed a lot of downtime when nothing was going on—no dancing and no music. He believed his club, the only black one in town, could be transformed into a winner. His fire was fueled by his anger at Ireland for not giving him the promised bonus and causing him to lose his farm to foreclosure. His son was born in August 1992, shortly after the farm was lost. The property was sold to an exclusive resort neighborhood and vineyard, Chateau Élan. Bitt lost the potential to make a lot of money in the sale. Another wedge between Bitt and Ireland occurred shortly after his son's birth. Bitt had never taken a vacation or time off, with the exception of his assignments for the government. He and Ireland verbally agreed that he would take a week off after the birth.

Banta experienced grueling labor with false contractions for about twenty-four hours before the delivery. When Bitt first saw his boy, he was overwhelmed with emotion and would always remember it as one of the most wonderful moments in his life. He called Ireland to give him the good news and told him he'd see him in a week. Ireland reacted poorly and told him he needed to come to work if he wanted to retain his job. The one night Bitt missed, when Banta was in labor, the club experienced a slow night, and Ireland panicked. Bitt gave his wife the bad news but promised her that he'd quit working for Ireland within a few months.

In order to keep his promise, Bitt needed to replenish his nest egg of cash. A few weeks later, he drove his truck to Fort Lauderdale by himself and took care of his money shortage. He scouted out some drug boys at a local club with the help of an old friend. His high school buddy who had teamed up with him to hijack the truckload of beef years earlier told Bitt which of the drug dealers were successful and ripe for being relieved of some of their holdings. Bitt's friend identified a couple of guys who typically carried a lot of money and usually had a couple of kilos of cocaine in the trunks of their cars. Bitt used a gun for these meetings and held up the two targets in the parking lot of Solid Gold that night. He robbed a third dealer at another site. His haul was significant: four kilos of cocaine, two Rolex watches, and $50,000 in cash. He moved the cocaine and the watches quickly and ended up with a total of $150,000. He hung on to the money and waited for the next opportunity to buy his way out of his relationship with Ireland. It soon materialized in the form of a customer who began showing up regularly at Norman's, Benson Signet Sr.

He started coming into the club and spending money as if it were going out of style. A self-styled cowboy from Nashville, Tennessee, Signet was in the process of moving to Atlanta and began to frequent Norman's. The amount of cash he distributed to the employees caught Bitt's attention, and Bitt began watching him closely while at the same time making sure he had whatever and whoever he wanted so he would tip generously. He came in every night for two weeks and acted like a human ATM. He purchased breast-enhancement surgeries for two of the dancers and bought a round for the house two to three times a night. Bitt was catering food for Signet every night and making sure he had everything he wanted. Signet was spending thousands of dollars a night in tabs and tips, but Bitt felt something was wrong with the situation. He had a notion that something was off in Signet's life, as he showed no big-shot bravado while spending so freely. Bitt didn't know why, but he was experiencing a feeling of guilt for taking advantage of a nice guy. He also found himself uncharacteristically worried about Signet's well-being. The Holy Spirit was likely whispering softly in Bitt's ear.

One night, in the middle of another Signet wild spending spree, Bitt asked him to come into his club office with him. Signet, who had come to like Bitt, agreed to go to the secluded room. Bitt closed the office door and asked Signet if he was a multimillionaire. He quickly replied to Bitt that his wife had recently died. He further explained that he was spending everything he'd received in death benefits from his wife's insurance policies. Bitt was moved to tears and would later realize that this was God nudging him and showing him there was still hope and redemption for him. In the past, Bitt would have drained every dollar he could out of Signet's pockets—but not this time. He asked Signet what he was going to do after he spent all of the money. Signet replied that he didn't know. He then told Bitt all about his wife of forty years, who'd died of cancer. He repeatedly told Bitt that she was the love of his life, he was lost without her, and he didn't care about himself. Bitt, not entirely moved to the point that he wasn't searching for another angle, asked Signet how much money he had left. Signet replied that he still had about $165,000. This was despite the fact that he had been routinely shelling out $10,000 to $15,000 a night at the club for a few weeks. Bitt told him he wasn't going to let him into the club for the next three nights, and he was going to save his life. The wheels were once again rolling in Bitt's head, as he figured he now had access to the rest of the money he needed to exit from Norman's.

After telling Signet to go back to his hotel room and sit tight, he asked for a meeting with Ireland and Lombopolus. He told them he wanted to buy the club in Augusta. They struck a deal for Bitt to purchase the club for $165,000. Signet provided the money to Bitt. Ireland didn't realize how quickly Norman's would drop in its revenues when Bitt left. Shortly thereafter, Bitt called a pimp and put together a load of girls to take to Augusta. A week later, Bitt and Signet left for Augusta with two carloads of girls and staff. He bought 250 nights at a local LaQuinta Inn in Augusta for thirty-two dollars per night in up-front cash. These rooms were where the dancers and a few of the staff stayed. Many of the dancers were attractive black ladies. Bitt found that the club had been mismanaged. He fired the entire staff except for two bouncers, Pokie 1 and Pokie 2. The site had to be remodeled, and that afforded a chance to get rid of all of the hookers and pimps who had set up shop in and around it. Bitt retained only one other former associate, James Lewis. He was important because he was the license holder for the business.

CHAPTER 18

The club was nasty in Bitt's estimation, and he used the $150,000 acquired on his three-day trip to Fort Lauderdale to update it. He had VIP rooms built to allow for one-on-one encounters with a dancer and a bottle of champagne. Signet, who was formerly a plumber and electrician, settled into the nightclub ownership life. Bitt also hired another Atlanta friend to come to Augusta to help him clear out the pimps and oversee the remodeling of the club over the first few months. Bitt changed the name of the establishment to Dolls Downtown and had neon lights installed on the outside. In addition to VIP rooms, he bought new carpet and built a couple of stages. He used a lot of polished wood to give the club a manly look. A few associates of Lewis came on board, including a short-statured lady named Kathryn. Bitt found Kathryn to be a smart woman and an asset to the business. He built a minibar at the front door, and she ran it. Customers entered and were required to buy two drinks when they came through the door. Bitt used a clicker in each hand and tracked the activities to be sure no one stole from the tills. Kathryn was in charge of taking money at the door for the cover charge and the minimum two drinks.

Business began to roll in as Bitt proved his CEO-worthy stature and knack for putting together and running a successful nightclub. However, his tenure in Augusta would be rocky at best. Even while the club was still being remodeled and was not yet open for business, he had an immediate issue. The pimps were angry at being run off of the corner near the club and sent a local thug to give Bitt an attitude adjustment. A man called Bear came to see Bitt. Bear had played big-time college football for a short stint at the University of Southern California and had been active in the parking lot at the Speak Easy, a.k.a. Dolls Downtown. Bear was already known to Bitt for beating up patrons in the parking lot and asking them for money to prevent their cars from being damaged. Bear walked into the club while the contractors were doing remodeling work and asked for Bitt. He was cracked up, and he found Bitt and spit in his face. Bitt leaped over the bar, and the tussle was on. The fight included punching, kicking, and gouging. It moved from the club to the parking lot and continued.

Five police cars arrived on the scene, and the officers clearly expected to see another guy being pummeled by Bear. They were surprised to find Bitt holding his own, but neither combatant was able to get the upper hand. After viewing the action for a short time, the police officers began striking Bear and Bitt with ash batons, small clubs with steel balls on the end of them. They were hitting both fighters from head to toe. Bitt was to later learn that it was illegal to use these instruments above the neck. When Bitt and Bear were thrown into two different cells, a strange sound came from the cell block. Bear was shaking his cell bars and yelling Bitt's name. He then screamed out, "Bitt, you're a good man!" Bitt didn't know how to take that or even figure out if it was a compliment. As Bitt would realize later, it was a compliment.

The police quickly discovered that Bitt was still on parole in Florida, which didn't bode well for him. They threatened to return him to Florida to face incarceration. Bitt contacted Lewis, who hired an attorney to represent him. The counselor was Judge Bergnon, a former local judge. Bergnon informed the police that he was prepared to represent Bitt and Bear and bring legal action against them for striking his clients above the shoulders with ash batons. He demanded that the charges against both men be dropped. The city government reluctantly agreed, and Bitt dodged a bullet. The last thing he wanted was to be sent back to Florida. Bitt made two good friends, Judge Bergnon and Bear. He hired Bear to manage the club's parking lot. He bought him some new clothes and allowed him to charge two dollars a car to watch over them while the owners were in the club. His shirt had "Parking Lot" stenciled on it. He also kept all of the crackheads and other undesirables away. Bear got clean, and Bitt raised his per-car allowance to five dollars. After about six months, Bear's drug problem reappeared, and he disappeared. Unfortunately, Bitt had made himself persona non grata with the police department over the ash-baton issue, and that would come back to haunt him.

Bitt's club was flourishing after about eight months and became a first-class joint. With Bear gone, he hired off-duty police officers for security outside of the club. He paid them twenty-five to thirty-five dollars an hour. He had other security on the inside of the club with him and really turned the business around. Bitt started bringing in feature acts in an attempt to draw more customers, both black and white. He utilized a connection with a South

Florida pimp who brought his cadre of girls into the club to help it get off the ground. Bitt did his part by hiring well-known porn stars, usually in groups of two, to draw in customers. At first, they were black performers, but Bitt began to bring in white girls too. Bitt paid $1,500 to $3,500 for these acts, and huge crowds lined up to get into Dolls Downtown to see them. He also advertised the acts in local newspapers to draw more customers. The soldiers at Fort Gordon patronized the club. Ever the entrepreneur, Bitt hired a photographer to take pictures of his customers with the porn stars. They cost the customers twenty-five dollars, and Bitt made ten dollars per shot. His expenses were about $1.50 per Polaroid. He made as much as $1,700 a night from photographs alone.

Signet acted like most of the owners Bitt knew and slept with most of the dancers and acts hired in the club. He was happy, but Bitt treated him more like a child than a man and later felt guilty that he didn't allow him to make more money. Bitt began bleeding into the white market by mixing black, white, and Latino dancers and acts. He soon had the number-one club in Augusta. The dancers and porn acts were also turning tricks for some of the customers. Just around the corner loomed a new money-making proposition for Bitt in the form of a most unlikely partner, the Masters Golf Tournament.

By February of 1994, Bitt was running a successful club, when he learned that the Masters Golf Tournament at Augusta National drew 250,000 guys a day into Augusta during a ten-day period each April. Downtown Dolls was just down the street from the course, and Bitt saw the potential to make some real money. Ever one to keep a close eye on his business, he knew there were some groundskeepers from Augusta National drinking in his club on a frequent basis. Bitt had his staff drive them home several times a week. He tried to extend his deal with LaQuinta for the rooms he was using into the summer, but the manager told him he couldn't let him have them during the week of the golf tournament. He also told him that he charged $300 a night during the tournament. More dollar signs appeared in Bitt's head upon his processing this information.

Back at Dolls, he asked the few holdover employees who'd worked for the previous owners what happened during the week of the tournament. They told him they closed the club and took a vacation. They further explained that the tournament drew primarily white middle-aged men, and they weren't interested in a black nightclub. Bitt was stunned to hear this, and plans began to take shape in his head. He knew he could draw white customers with a blended group of dancers and feature acts. He did some research and contacted Universal Entertainment and a few other organizations that provided dancers, and he asked if some house girls were available. These would be girls who would wait on tables, perform lap dances, and work with the twenty or so girls Bitt regularly employed to perform these tasks. At the time, Dolls Downtown was pulling in $20,000 to $25,000 a week in revenues, $40,000 in a strong week. Bitt had low overhead in that he was the janitor, stocker, and manager. His monthly rent was only $800. He continued to consistently track the incoming customers on his clicker to be sure no one was stealing from him.

He was uncertain what to expect when tournament week came around, but he arranged for about twenty feature acts starring black dancers and a few white ones. His employees were also learning from him how to treat customers with respect, even the thugs. Bitt welcomed customers from all walks of life and made friends with nearly everyone he met. The club became a safer environment than it had been in the past, which led to stability. Bitt brought in acts from across the country through Universal during the week of the tournament. He paid them $1,000 for the week and arranged for their lodging by renting out five local houses for up to $3,500 a week. He told the homeowners he was running a security company. He put up six or more girls in each house for the week.

The first year was a learning experience for Bitt during tournament week. He rented a large outdoor sign with flashing arrows and secured it into the bed of his truck. He then had an employee drive the truck up and down Washington Avenue so patrons and others could read the following message: "Dolls Downtown, Washington Avenue. Girls, girls, girls!" He also took the acts to eat at various restaurants in town to draw interest by parading the groups of beautiful women in front of the out-of-town men and conversing with them at the bar. He even used his employees and dancers to hand out flyers at apartments, on the golf course, and at competing nightclubs. These marketing ploys worked wonders. The first tournament during which the club stayed open for business brought in $162,000. Bitt was convinced he left at least that much money on the table by not being as efficient as he could have been. The expenses for the week were a little more than $100,000, but he still made a tidy profit of more than $60,000. More importantly, he learned what to do and how to do it better next year. The girls made as much as $20,000 in addition to the $1,000 Bitt paid them to show up. Accordingly, the word spread among the performers, and he had no problem finding dancers for tourney week during the years that followed. After his first Masters week, Bitt knew the annual event was going to be a slam dunk for Dolls Downtown.

In the years to follow, dancers begged him to be allowed to participate and sent him their portfolios with résumés and photographs. Bitt had heard that during the week of the golf tournament, there were more millionaires per square mile present in town than anywhere else. There were Fortune 500 company executives, celebrities, and athletes in Augusta each year. Even Bill Gates would show up on occasion. Bitt could hear the cash register ringing in his head. He met Michael Jordan, Charles Barkley, and Tiger Woods during one tournament, when they rented a local house together. Bitt provided them with groups of dancers for entertainment purposes in groups of six to eight at a time. Bitt had an employee pick up and drop off girls for the trio during the week of the tournament on a twenty-four-hour basis. Woods was, of course, playing in the event during the daytime hours.

Over time, Bitt built more VIP rooms with doors that could be closed for privacy. He had a dozen of them installed in the basement of the club. None of the other nightclubs offered these types of services or even outside security. Bitt was living in Augusta during the Masters in 1994, 1995, and 1996. Dolls Downtown drew a lot of business from the caddies carrying clubs for the golfing pros. A few other golfers came into the club, most notably John Daly. One day during one of the tournaments, Daly came into the club and asked for a beer. Bitt, who didn't recognize him at first, told him the club wasn't open yet, but then he realized who was standing in front of him. Daly stayed, drank beer, and didn't leave till closing time. On another occasion, Daly asked Bitt if he would cash a $10,000 check from a sponsor for him. Bitt replied that he would rather loan him the money than take a check, and he also offered him complimentary drinks and services in Dolls Downtown.

Bitt found that the golfers in the Masters received generous gift bags with watches, clothes, and more. He set up an arrangement in which the golfers could send their caddies to Bitt and arrange for a girl or two for company during that evening. The caddies would show Bitt their tournament badges, which allowed them access to the golf course and areas off limits to the general public. Comfortable that he was not sending any girls into harm's way, Bitt would then broker a deal with the caddies. After receiving the agreed-upon cash payment, he arranged for a dancer or two to be driven to the particular house being rented by the requesting athlete. Bitt's rates for the personal services of the girls were a minimum of $1,000 to make up for the money he would lose due to the dancer's absence during the evening.

Over the next few years, the profitability of Masters week for the club skyrocketed. Bitt started bringing in up to 150 girls for the week and spent $100,000 just to house them for seven days. By Wednesday, the club was in the black for the week. The VIP rooms were in demand, and all twelve of the ones in the basement and the one in the main floor were constantly in use. The cover charge to get in would rise in direct correlation to the demand. It would often start out at ten dollars and reach a hundred dollars as customers lined up, waiting to get in. Bitt made arrangements to have limousines available to transport girls and customers, and he also rented three mobile homes, which he parked across the street from Dolls Downtown. He was wired with some of the local cops at the time, and he hired ten off-duty police officers to escort dancers and customers across the street to the mobile homes for personal attention.

Bitt paid the head of vice in the Augusta Police Department, Stoney Turnage, to leave him and his club alone. He considered this to be a cost of doing business, but the terms kept changing. Turnage constantly asked for more money and other forms of compensation in addition to the $10,000 to $15,000 he demanded during the course of the year. Bitt also arranged for Turnage to receive Masters tickets and even purchased his wife a new washer and dryer one year, another cost of doing business. Turnage went too far with Bitt when he stopped Bitt's wife and son in a traffic stop. Turnage and his officers removed the tires from the car and disassembled parts of it, ostensibly looking for drugs. Bitt didn't forget that, and it drove a permanent wedge between Bitt and his wife at that time. His payback time would come a few years down the road. By that time, Bitt was in the process of building and opening a sports bar, and he expected Turnage would make a play for more protection money.

CHAPTER 19

In 1995, Bitt's new sports bar was being built on the site of a former Western Sizzlin' Restaurant. He loaded it up with TVs and sports memorabilia, spending in excess of $600,000. It was beautiful when finished and was the closest facility to Augusta National with a liquor license. The establishment represented Bitt's first attempt to do something legitimate outside of the nightclub industry. He was attending a small local church by himself and felt an urge to get out of the girlie business. No one at the church spoke to him or made an attempt to form a relationship, but Bitt yearned to transition into a regular business owner. He was still under pressure from the DEA, CIA, and FBI to do more undercover jobs, as the legal charges in Florida were still pending, as was the threat of extradition. They kept him hanging for years, constantly asking him for information and trying to insert him into sting operations. He consistently refused to help them with anything he thought was related to organized crime. Bitt was involved in about thirty undercover assignments for various agencies over the years. Meanwhile, Augusta PD's Turnage continued to throw road blocks in Bitt's path while trying to further line his own pockets.

At the time, Bitt wanted to clean his life up, and he saw the sports bar as an avenue to accomplish this. His wife was raising their son and dancing at a club in nearby South Carolina occasionally for fun and extra money. Dolls Downtown, to Bitt's chagrin, essentially became a house of prostitution during the week of the Masters, and it made him feel dirty. His sports bar was his chance to turn his life around. He put a lot of effort into it and spared no expense. It had hardwood floors from the United Center in Chicago, where the Chicago Bulls played. He had several fifty-two-inch TVs in the club. For the first time, Bitt's family came to see him for Christmas in 1995. He showed his mother, sisters, and other relatives the bar that was nearing the end of the construction process. He was proud of the interior, including the 1,500 pieces of sports memorabilia, which consisted of bats, balls, pictures, autographs, signed jerseys, and other items. The sports bar became the most important project of Bitt's life and, he hoped, his pathway to a respectable livelihood.

Bitt hired a chef from a local Outback Steakhouse to allow his establishment to offer more than the usual bar fare. He gave the chef a big raise over his current salary and a small piece of the place. Little did he know that the chef would turn on him in the future. Bitt hired a real-estate executive to secure all of the necessary licenses he needed to open the bar. He purchased a new car for her in return for her assistance. Bitt put almost all of his money into the sports bar and brought Josh Douglas on board to be his front man. Coming from a local Augusta nightspot, Chevy's, Douglas agreed to be the general manager and owner in name only because Bitt couldn't put his own name in the paperwork and license applications due to his criminal background. Douglas, from a local well-to-do family, also got a small piece of the club to be called the Dugout Sports Bar. Bitt had visions of buying the local minor-league baseball team if the bar was successful.

Bitt booked seven former New York Yankee stars for the opening of the Dugout in January 1996. He also bought a museum-worthy pictorial display from a dealer in New York of the famous Babe Ruth home run in which he pointed to the outfield wall. The *Augusta Chronicle* did a feature on all of the baseball lore Bitt purchased. Shortly before the opening of the bar, Turnage visited Bitt and informed him that he knew he was the money behind building the bar, and he wasn't going to let him open. Bitt stuck with his story that the seed money came from the other owners, but the city pulled the necessary licensure. Dolls Downtown's license was also suspended, although it was reinstated by the local court after about six months of legal maneuvering. The competing local nightclubs were pressing the politicians and the law enforcement powers to close Bitt down because he was taking so much of their business. Augusta had never seen the approach Bitt used to draw in customers to his club. The only negative as far as Bitt was concerned was that he was responsible for an upscale red-light district as well as a club. This was the biggest reason he wanted to open and operate a successful sports bar. He wanted to abandon the seedier nature of the nightclub industry and become a bar owner with no dancers or acts.

However, Turnage was willing to forego his $500 weekly payments from Bitt to close down Dolls Downtown. Bitt was broke, and he wasn't able to open the bar. By March 1996, Bitt had resorted to trying to run Dolls Downtown as a juice bar, which didn't work. As a result, Dolls Downtown became a year-round house of ill repute, offering cheap accommodations in the form of VIP rooms. Bitt was becoming disgusted with the situation but felt he was forced into this approach when he couldn't get his liquor license reinstated. Then Turnage came to Bitt and informed him that he'd decided to let him open Dugout. However, there was a catch: Turnage wanted 50 percent of the receipts each and every night. Bitt became angry and told Turnage what he thought of him despite the fact that he was the head of the vice department. He didn't agree to the demand, and another agreement was eventually reached. Bitt signed a written agreement with the county sheriff stipulating that he would never set foot in the sports bar for any reason. He was desperate to open and signed the agreement against his better judgment. Unfortunately, all of the staff soon turned against Bitt. He blamed Turnage for their turnabout. Bitt was refused access to the records of the bar by the people he had hired. He wasn't even allowed access to the sports memorabilia he had purchased and put on display.

After six months of operations with no oversight by Bitt, the Dugout Sports Bar closed. Bitt's dream was dead. He was particularly upset with Ralph Miller, who was lucky he never crossed paths with Bitt after the closure. To his surprise, Bitt was eventually able to get inside the club to recover the majority of his sports memorabilia. He wasn't above partaking in a scam at any time, and while the bar was being remodeled for its opening, a windfall fell into his lap. A Hilton Head resident who'd previously lived in Augusta and owned nightclubs and arranged concerts approached Bitt through Josh Douglas. Bitt was used to people making runs at him to buy drugs, usually cocaine. Douglas's request came at a time when Bitt was in need of cash since the bar was not yet open, and Dolls Downtown was struggling with licensure issues. Bitt set a hook in the requester and told him it would cost $58,000 for two kilos of cocaine. The buyer insisted on sending a local bodybuilder to carry the payment and receive the coke. Bitt, who had no intention of making good on the deal, said he was fine with the buyer sending an errand boy along for the ride.

Having no plan, Bitt met the young, well-muscled kid at eight o'clock in the morning in front of the under-construction Dugout. He told him to take a seat in the passenger side of his truck and plan to be gone for most of the day. The youngster, carrying a paper bag with the $58,000 in it, did as he was told. Bitt drove to

Atlanta, thinking along the way of how he was going to relieve the kid of the money he was toting. Using his likeability and friendly banter, he set about putting the youngster at ease. He took him to a sports memorabilia show organized by an acquaintance, Dexter Laddle. Bitt had met Laddle in years past when he donated to Toys for Tots and the Make-A-Wish Foundation. The show was in the basement of a now-closed Atlanta hotel, and Bitt introduced his young companion to Laddle and a couple of current Atlanta Braves. He then took him to a well-known nightclub for lunch. Everyone at the club hovered around Bitt, including the dancers, the bouncers, and Kevin Nash, a World Wrestling Federation champion. They ate and drank for three hours, and the youngster was impressed with Bitt's celebrity aura.

At four o'clock that afternoon, Bitt's cell phone rang. It was a prearranged call from his South Florida friend. Bitt answered his phone, listened for a few seconds, and asked the caller if he was going to meet him in the same spot. Receiving an affirmation to this question, Bitt told the caller he would see him in two hours, and he ended the conversation. He told his companion that the deal was going to go down in Conyers, Georgia, which was on the way back to Augusta. He further informed him that he had to get out of the truck for the meeting, but the young man said he couldn't leave the money. Bitt replied, "Fine. I'll call it off," and he took out his phone. He began punching some numbers in his cell, and the bodybuilder told him to stop. He said he couldn't come back without the coke. Bitt smiled at him; he had him hook, line, and sinker now. Bitt took the money, left the kid at a club, and departed. He drove to a Kmart and killed some time for twenty minutes. He then called his buddy in Florida back and related that they were going to be calling each other back and forth, screaming at each other. His coconspirator agreed, and Bitt went back to the club where the kid was waiting. First, he put the money under the driver's seat in his truck. The youngster was worried and asked Bitt where he'd gone and if he had the coke. Without answering him, Bitt made a call and asked what was wrong and why his accomplice had driven off from the meeting site. Per Bitt's previous instructions, his friend began screaming loudly in Spanish, and Bitt yelled back at him. Bitt's friend hung up on him, and the bodybuilder became very worried. Bitt called his dealer back three times and engaged in yelling sessions, and each time, the other party hung up on Bitt. Bitt called a few more times, and no one answered. The young would-be coke purchaser was now in panic mode. He thought Bitt had given the money to the seller and was distraught. He eventually called his boss in Hilton Head and told him what he thought had occurred. Bitt then gave the kid a quiet ride home with the $58,000 under his seat.

A week later, the buyer drove from Hilton Head to Augusta and looked up Bitt. He asked exactly what had happened, and Bitt told him the truth. He informed him that he'd needed the money and taken it. He further told the would-be buyer that he should conduct business himself and not send someone so weak to do it for him. He asked Bitt what he was going to do about it, and Bitt turned the question around, asking him what he was going to do about it. The Hilton Head man said the botched transaction had really hurt him financially, and Bitt, ever the wheeler and dealer, made the following offer. He told him that the going rate for a kilo of coke was $28,000 to $32,000. He said he would sell him up to eleven kilos at cost for $22,000 each. In reality, Bitt was setting him up. He arranged for FBI agents to be present in the parking lot of the buyer's Hilton Head restaurant in a sting operation. Bitt was actually settling a score with the buyer for a slight that had occurred a few months earlier. Bitt had taken his wife and son to Hilton Head for a few days on the beach. The restaurant owner had come to meet Bitt at his beachfront hotel and been enamored with Mrs. Thrower. He'd stared at her, unable to take his eyes off of her. He'd hit on her while Bitt played pitch and catch with his son a few feet away.

Bitt didn't get mad, but he did get even to the tune of $58,000 and setting him up to be arrested for a second attempted drug buy. Ironically, the feds told Bitt he could keep $3,000 for each kilo that was to be sold, so he picked up an extra $15,000 on top of the $58,000 he had previously stolen. Bitt had set up the arrest through his old GBI contact, Douglas Donlan. The takedown involved local FBI agents because the GBI had no jurisdictional authority in South Carolina. The day before the would-be buyer's trial was scheduled, Donlan called Bitt and asked him if he had left out anything of the story he had told him. Bitt said no, but Donlan inquired if he had robbed the target. Bitt admitted that he had done so. This cog in the wheel led to the charges against the restaurant owner being dismissed, and Bitt never heard from him again. He worked several more Masters Tournaments, bringing in hookers and dancers each year to boost club revenues. He also purchased a small Augusta nightclub, Club 24. It opened its doors at 2:00 a.m. and closed when the last customer left. The sheriff hated the fact that Club 24 was open all night. It was bringing in about $15,000 a week for only fifteen hours of operation. Law enforcement officials threatened to block all access to the club with squad cars but eventually relinquished, agreeing to allow it to continue operations for three more months if it would then shut its doors. Bitt agreed to this arrangement, and he sold Club 24 for $70,000 a few weeks later to some South Carolina dope dealers, ridding him of a headache. The sheriff then closed the club down a few weeks after the sale as a result of applying pressure to the new owners.

Bitt's wife and son moved back to the Atlanta area in mid-1996. Bitt recovered the liquor license for Dolls Downtown, and it once again became profitable. He saved most of the money he made, putting away $200,000 in quick order. He had just finished another Masters week-long run, when he reached a handshake arrangement with James Lewis and became a silent partner in Dolls Downtown. He drove to Augusta on a monthly basis to pick up his share of the club earnings. He also returned to Augusta each April for the next nine years to coordinate the activities of the club during the Masters Tournament. He made tens of thousands of dollars each April, as well as his usual monthly nut from Lewis. Bitt stayed in Coco Beach, Florida, for a couple of months in 1996 to take a sabbatical from the business. He took his son with him, and they enjoyed the beach life. Even at that early age, his offspring displayed some of his dad's athleticism by hitting plastic baseballs a long way down the beach. During that time, Bitt listened to a pitch from a longtime South Florida pimp and two local club owners. They invited Bitt to manage a string of four Jacksonville clubs on a lease-type arrangement. Bitt went to each of the clubs to view their operations and look at their books. He turned down the offer because he decided he couldn't make any money after paying the three would-be investors what they wanted in payments each month.

CHAPTER 20

While taking his break between jobs, Bitt ran across an old acquaintance in an Orlando bar. The man recognized Bitt from playing softball with him years earlier in Atlanta. A friend and teammate of Thurston Taylor while playing for Florida State University and the Philadelphia Eagles, Big Boy was now in real estate, the diamond business, and the dope business. He took Bitt to some clubs, and they had a lively night. Bitt met a dancer to whom he was attracted, and they started meeting on weekends in Orlando, while he continued to stay in Coco Beach during the week. He went to some Orlando Magic games and hooked up with her on each trip, often staying at her house. During that time, Bitt and Big Boy made some money in the same manner he had earlier in the form of bait and switch. They found a couple of marks, and Bitt played the out-of-town drug supplier. They took in $64,000 in one evening at two bars, and Big Boy had no worries about retribution. He considered Orlando to be his town.

Bitt went home to Atlanta in mid-1996, and his soon-to-be ex-wife told him Bob Ireland had been trying to reach him. Bitt had already talked to Ireland before leaving Augusta, telling him he was interested in working for him again but needed a break, hence the two-month stay in Coco Beach. Bitt was now ready to get back in the game. He recommended Bodie Perez, the former DEA agent, to run Bob's lingerie stores. While Bitt was away, Bob had changed the name of Stormin' Norman's to Peaches. Bitt found Peaches to be in poor shape, from the condition of the property down to the less-than-impressive dancers and waitresses. The club was bringing in less than $15,000 a week. Bitt had no money problems at the time, as he had cash from his Augusta activities and his $32,000 share from the gig in Orlando with Big Boy. This time, Bitt asked for a contract with Ireland with bonus incentives tied to weekly revenues. The first bonus was to occur when Peaches hit weekly revenues of $50,000. On Bitt's first day, he held a mandatory meeting with the staff. He fired everyone but eight of the dancers and three of the waitresses. Ireland was upset, but Bitt told him to let him do his thing and trust him. At the time, he had a good street reputation because he hadn't flipped anyone, as he had in Orlando and Augusta.

It was another perfect storm for Bitt, as the Olympics were being hosted by the city of Atlanta. Bitt dressed up the club. He repainted everything and hired a gypsy crew to repave the parking lot. Bitt had a relationship with a local car dealer, Paul Winger, known as the Slasher. Winger held auctions in which there were five expensive cars among many used vehicles listed at only $200. When the painters had van troubles, Bitt promised them a used van. Winger was hooked on the VIP experience Bitt had provided for him at various clubs in the past. He agreed to inform selected auction patrons sent by Bitt which vehicles to pick for the $200 prize. The rest of the auction attendees were running around and vying for first dibs on cars and trucks, hoping their selection was one of the $200 ones sprinkled among the hundreds of possibilities. Bitt told Winger he needed a $200 van for the painting crew, and Winger made sure the Peaches employee Bitt sent to him knew the row and parking-spot number to rush to and claim an underpriced van. In this manner, Bitt paid a total of $286, including tax, for a work van, and the club was the recipient of a complete new coat of paint in exchange for it. To give the building a special look, Bitt and the employees blew glitter on the wet paint before it dried. The club was trimmed in red, white, and blue. After the gypsies resurfaced the parking lot, Bitt made a few inside improvements, including adding two more VIP rooms. He spent only $5,000 updating the property.

Using his reputation and contacts, Bitt picked up girls, bartenders, and waitresses from the Gold Club and other establishments. Located north of I-285, the club was ready for the Olympics, and within the first month of operation under Bitt, Peaches went from twenty-five to forty dancers and from four VIP rooms to ten. The atmosphere was cleaner than Dolls Downtown, and the revenues hit $50,000 within the first two months, earning Bitt a $5,000 bonus. Things turned around so quickly that Ireland invited Bitt to live in one of his houses, on Lake Lanier, in the exclusive Pilgrim Mill Circle subdivision. He had the use of a dock and a pontoon boat. Perez and his girlfriend lived in the basement. Bitt had visitation with his son every other weekend, and Perez kept a low profile when the boy was onsite. Bitt was living on his tips and asked that his bonuses be paid on a quarterly basis. He received one for $144,000. Clearly, Peaches was back in a big way. After a few months, the weekly revenues climbed into the $70,000 range, most of which was earned on the night shift. There were now one hundred dancers and waitresses on board. Bitt was the general manager and security man and a keen observer of the customers. He again hired local cops for parking lot security, and the club began drawing celebrities and athletes, including several of the Atlanta Braves.

One regular customer was Atlanta Hawks point guard Mookie Blaylock. One night, he was sitting at the bar, obviously under the influence. He was accused by another customer of stealing thirty dollars from him. Bitt didn't know who he was but had noticed his expensive clothes and willingness to throw around a lot of money. He compensated the complaining customer in drinks and food worth considerably more than thirty dollars. He then struck up a conversation with Blaylock and learned that he was an NBA player who had also been a Division I star at Oklahoma University. Bitt told him he wanted to provide him a cab ride home because of his inebriated condition. Blaylock got in the cab but quickly doubled back, took his keys from the valet, and screeched the tires of his juiced-up Mustang all the way out of the parking lot. Blaylock became a regular and hung out with Bitt and the other employees at the bar. He wasn't interested in the girls, but Bitt and his staff came to like him for his humble nature. Bitt also admired him for his tenacious defensive ability on the basketball court. Unfortunately, years later, he was involved in a head-on collision in Atlanta while under the influence and was held responsible for the death of a woman in the other car. He was sentenced to fifteen years in prison, which was reduced to three years to be followed by probation upon release.

Peaches grew to the point that Bitt had to hire a manager to help him with the paperwork. He oversaw the installation of surveillance cameras and a thumb-print device for documentation of signatures on bar tabs. This prevented customers from claiming that they'd lost their credit cards or someone else had used it to run up big charges. The popularity of Peaches grew as Bitt loosened things up by allowing some of the waitresses and dancers to provide services to customers in the VIP rooms. He coordinated many of these trysts for NFL players, who would flash their player ID cards and pay entertainment fees of $500 to $750. He also found different ways to increase the club's profit margin. He began purchasing a few Cuban cigars and removed the labels. The day manager would then copy the labels on a high-quality printer and cut them into appropriate-sized strips. He then glued them onto cigars he purchased from Sam's that cost much less than expensive imported ones. He supplied these fake Cuban cigars to VIP customers. He also used some of his old tried-and-true strategies, such as using limousines to pick up some of the customers or drop them off at their homes or a hotel room. From 1996 through early 2003, Peaches was a money-making jewel. It seated 155, but there were typically three hundred or more people packed into it. For weekend crowds, Bitt even put up black curtains in the doorways of the administrative offices for makeshift VIP rooms.

One night in the late '90s, Bitt saw a large, well-dressed man walking from table to table in the club, engaging the customers in conversation. Initially thinking he was an NFL player due to his size, Bitt asked Boomer, his manager, to tell him who the gentleman was. He learned that the giant man was a drug dealer, so Bitt pulled him into a back room and told him to empty his pockets onto a table. The man didn't want to, so Bitt and Boomer tuned him up. After he regained consciousness, the dealer coughed up a load of coke, pills, and marijuana from inside his pockets and even in his socks. Bitt then ordered him to strip completely. Bitt and the manager perp-walked him through the club in front of the patrons. Bitt grabbed the microphone from the deejay and announced to the crowd, "You're always welcome to party at Peaches, but if you try to sell drugs here, this is what you're gonna get." Bitt and Boomer then walked the large naked man through the club a second time before kicking him out sans clothes.

The dealer ran over to La Paz, a restaurant next door, and some workers in the alley gave him a pair of spandex shorts. In the meantime, a local mob-connected man pulled up to Peaches in his Maserati and told Bitt he had received a call from someone in the club. He said he'd come over to see what was going on. He asked if there was any video of what had happened. Before he could answer, someone told Bitt the dealer had acquired some pants, and Bitt went next door behind La Paz to check it out. He demanded that the already-embarrassed dealer remove the shorts or face another beating. He did as ordered and took off. He next ran to a nearby adult bookstore and asked patrons for any articles of clothes they were willing to part with. Soon the police were called, and they paid Bitt a visit a short time later. The officer asked Bitt if he had the man's clothes, and he said he did. When the officer asked why he'd taken them, Bitt replied that the man was a drug dealer. The cop wanted to know where the drugs were, and Bitt replied that he and his employees had flushed them down the toilet, which was true. He asked for the dealer's clothes and money back, and Bitt gave them to him. The cop told Bitt he had to cite him for false imprisonment before he handed the clothing and money to the naked man in the back of the police car. Bitt appeared in the Fulton County Court several days later, but the dealer didn't show up. The judge told Bitt she had been looking forward to hearing the case of the naked dope dealer. She then asked Bitt to approach the bench. She requested that he please keep the clothes on any drug dealers he encountered in the future and turn them in to the authorities. Bitt agreed to do so and left the courthouse.

CHAPTER 21

Jamal Anderson, the Atlanta Falcons running back, followed an old NFL tradition by taking his offensive line out to eat in appreciation for blocking for him. One Friday night, Anderson took some of his teammates to eat at a LongHorn Steakhouse and then brought them to Peaches. This became a weekly routine, and it coincided with a Falcons winning streak. Near the end of the season, there were twenty-five Falcons frequenting the club on Friday nights prior to the games on Sundays. One of the players in attendance was a rookie linebacker named Keith Brookings. It just so happened that Brookings had played high school football with one of Bitt's brothers. After a short time, Bitt and Brookings bonded. Bitt instructed the girls in the club not to rush the players but to let them talk among themselves and wait to see if they were interested in female companionship. Midway through the season, the Falcons decided to try the Gold Club on Friday night instead of Peaches. They were then beaten soundly by the New York Giants on Sunday. On Monday, Anderson called Bitt and told him to save their spots on Friday night. Bitt realized some huge tabs from the players, as much as $10,000 to $15,000 on some nights from Anderson. On one occasion, Anderson asked Bitt to reverse the charges on his American Express, and he began to pay for his fun with cash. Bitt was, of course, happy with any form of currency.

By 2003, Bitt had led Peaches to being among the top Atlanta clubs in champagne sales week in and week out. He had accumulated a seven-digit stash by that time and now had the funds to buy a club on his own. Ireland made it clear he wasn't going to offer him an ownership interest in Peaches. Bitt was interested in a club called the Hot Spot and, more recently, Platinum. It was destined to be renamed Platinum 21 by Bitt. Ireland purchased the club with the assistance of a friend of Bitt's, Shane Garvin. The former owner operated a string of gas stations and was also a farmer. Garvin was a retired Bell South employee but later became a drug dealer and a self-proclaimed part-time hit man. He dabbled in sports memorabilia but always wanted a piece of a club. He desired to team up with Bitt because he knew Bitt could turn clubs around and make them profitable. Garvin worked for Bitt in Augusta and helped provide girls to golfers and others during the week of the Masters Tournament. His nickname was the Dream Maker. He had the reputation of being able to make any request connected to the adult entertainment world come to fruition.

Prior to 2000, Garvin received an offer from two local thugs to kill Bitt. They filled vending machines for a living and kept asking Bitt to help them buy drugs. He took money from them for a kilo of cocaine, decided to keep it, and dared them to do something about it. The price they offered Garvin to do away with Bitt was a paltry $2,500. Garvin told the two cheapskates that they needed to come up with more money if they wanted someone of Bitt's stature taken down. Garvin told Bitt about the offer, and they shared a laugh over it.

The agreed-upon purchase price for the Hot Spot was $1.5 million. Bitt told Ireland of his plan and invited him to buy it with him. Naturally, Ireland didn't want Bitt to leave Peaches. He knew Bitt had the funds to make the purchase, so he agreed to join in on the purchase if the profits were evenly shared. Ireland put up

45 percent of the money, Bitt put up 45 percent, and the rest was provided by an influential local judge and attorney. After he and Ireland acquired Platinum 21, Bitt spent time at both Peaches and the new venue. Over the next two years, Peaches started dropping off in its popularity.

Platinum 21 was a black club and did well. Bitt was proud that the club was mentioned by name in several rap songs, as Atlanta was and is the rapper capital of America. Shortly after purchasing the club, Bitt remodeled the building after a suspicious fire allowed him to avoid some building-code restrictions and increase the height of the ceiling. He again painted everything, including the floors. He spent about $300,000 in improvements, and his share of the purchase price was financed and quickly paid off. Platinum 21 was close to the Onyx club, owned by Jack Glory, on the edge of downtown Atlanta and Buckhead. Platinum 21 became the hangout for the Black Mafia Family, a.k.a. the BMF. They were a drug-dealing gang, and they tattooed numbers on their necks in pecking-order number of their importance. Their members included the rapper Jeezy. Bitt remodeled a storage room in the basement of Platinum 21, making it a special VIP room for the BMF only. They were a rough crowd, and Bitt hired one of their members to handle BMF's parties and its relationship with the club. This go-between was later shot and killed at Platinum 21.

There was no sex or girlie action at Platinum 21. It was a drinking, drug-dealing Wild West place. Floyd Mayweather and other patrons frequently tossed fifty to a hundred dollars in ones at dancers in the club. BMF would come into the club after hours on the weekends, after the 2:00 a.m. closing time. They parked in the rear and entered a back door to go to their basement VIP room. BMF would pay Bitt $10,000 an hour for their early morning events. They purchased a lot of champagne and held private parties. There were lots of girls present, who made a lot of tip money, which was shared, of course, with Bitt. He typically stayed at Peaches until midnight and then went to Platinum 21 for the late-night activities. The dancers for Platinum 21 were primarily black. They unanimously wanted nothing to do with any white or Hispanic fellow entertainers.

Bitt was still struggling with his spiritual well-being. By that time, he'd been attending a Baptist church in Cumming, Georgia, for about seven years. He attended the worship services two to three times a month and usually put up to $500 in the offering plate, depending on how much cash he was carrying. He took his son and stepson to services with him but made a point to avoid too much interaction with the church members. Eventually, the pastor of the church and the youth minister began talking with Bitt and encouraged him to put his lifestyle behind him and embrace the Lord. However, Bitt thought he was beyond redemption and was hoping he could broker a deal with God to keep his boys from following in his footsteps. He prayed to Jesus, saying he would bring the boys to church and give significant money to it to protect his children. He even arranged a courtesy limousine service a couple of times for some of the youth of the church for prom transportation. However, he was not ready to consider changing his ways and continued to live at a break-neck pace. He enjoyed the money, but more than that, he was addicted to the power, prestige, and sex readily at his disposal. He began to insist on having at least two girls at a time be with him, and he coined a phrase he used with potential lovers: "It takes a pair or better to open." Most of the time, the objects of his desire were more than happy to be his selections. Platinum 21 represented a new level of excitement for Bitt, as it ushered him into the world of the black criminal community in Atlanta, acclimating him to the violence and hip-hop lifestyle that went along with it. However, deep down, he knew he was drifting further away from the Lord.

In 1997, Bitt's marriage to Janice Banta was on the rocks and essentially over in all but name. Both sides were ready to move on, and he decided it was time to file for divorce. A friend of Bitt's suggested he secure the services of a Cumming attorney. The acquaintance was a retired state trooper who had worked on the security detail for four Georgia governors. He recommended Bitt hire Mike Ernest III, Esq. Ernest was formerly the district attorney in Forsyth County and a well-known criminal law attorney. His friend instructed Bitt to put $20,000 in a bag and take it with him when he went to Ernest's office. Bitt showed up without an appointment and told the receptionist who had sent him. She called Ernest on the intercom, and he came into the reception area. Bitt said he was a friend of a friend, and Ernest took him back into his office. When Bitt told him he wanted representation in a divorce matter, Ernest was polite but firm when he told Bitt he didn't handle divorce cases. Bitt liked Ernest immediately and told him that money was no object if he would agree to take the case. Again, Ernest declined. Bitt told him he had $20,000 with him and would double or triple that amount if Ernest would represent him. Ernest turned him down again, explaining that he never took divorce cases. Bitt was disappointed but shook hands with Ernest and left.

A couple of weeks later, Bitt received a phone call at the lake house. It was Ernest. He told Bitt that he didn't know what kind of relationship he had with their mutual friend, but he'd just been accosted by a three-hundred-pound man in the nearby Cherokee County Courthouse. He shared that the intimidating giant had strongly suggested he reconsider representing Bitt in his divorce case. He told Bitt this was going to be the last divorce he ever handled, but he wanted him in his office tomorrow morning. He also reminded Bitt to bring the bag of cash. Ernest did a stellar job for Bitt and helped him win full custody of his son. His estranged wife brought in several witnesses, including James Lewis, Bitt's partner in Augusta. She also subpoenaed others she knew had been involved in drug deals and other criminal enterprises with Bitt. Of course, all of them were smart enough to be careful of what they said to the judge, for fear of making Bitt mad at them. Therefore, no negative information passed from their lips in the courtroom. For his side, Bitt had a few police officers speak on his behalf, as well as presenting a dying declaration from a lady with terminal cancer who described his wife's less-than-upright lifestyle. Her witnesses also hurt her because they were open about her heavy drinking and carousing. Bitt presented a representative of the US Marine Corps, a gunnery sergeant, to verify Bitt's charity work for Toys for Tots at Peaches. In fact, there were two marines in dress uniforms on Bitt's side of the courtroom during each day of the divorce proceedings.

CHAPTER 22

In 2002, Bitt married Rhonda Woodard, his third and last wife. She was the mother of Bitt's third and fourth children, Kalie and Calie, twins who were born in 2003. This union officially ended when Woodard, a beautiful dancer and entertainer of black, white, and Puerto Rican descent, succumbed to cancer in 2012. Although he wasn't always living with her, Bitt took some time to smooth out his relationship with his natural daughter, Bella, who was now about sixteen years old. She was raised by her grandparents. Similar to what he'd done for his stepdaughter, Bitt arranged for her and her friends to be driven to concerts and school proms in limousines.

He also did one particularly special thing for his daughter and one of her good friends, Beth Ireland, the daughter of his partner and boss, Bob Ireland. Every year during the Christmas season, he purchased three or four tickets to *The Nutcracker* ballet at the regal Fox Theater in Atlanta and sent Bella, Beth, and one or two of their girlfriends to the show in a chauffeur-driven limo. Bella admired her father's generosity with friends and family. She was also impressed with his participation in donating to charitable organizations, such as the Make-A-Wish Foundation.

At four years old, Bella may have had a better read on Bitt than a lot of others, as evidenced by her steadfast belief that he was actually Steven Seagal. She would yell her belief out loud to other patrons at the local movie theater, much to the consternation of her mother. As she grew older and attended high school, she had to face ridicule from other students who called her dad a gangster or a murderer. It was hard on her when the other parents looked down on Bitt, who was always dressed in expensive clothes and driving luxury cars or trucks. Bella knew her father as a family man who was fiercely loyal to his parents, children, and relatives.

Platinum 21 became wildly successful as Bitt continued to employ his proven strategies of micromanaging the operations and treating the employees, particularly the dancers, with respect. He catered to them whenever possible to reduce turnover and increase the male patrons' satisfaction. He even built dressing rooms with single and double lockers in the basement of the club. This created incredible loyalty to Bitt. He solicited written suggestions from the dancers and staff and gave each submission serious consideration.

He continued to practice his P. T. Barnum approach to increase Platinum's visibility. He allowed up-and-coming bands to play one night a week at the club. He kept hiring most of his deejays from local radio stations, which produced a lot of free advertising on their local radio programs when they plugged the club during their broadcasts. Bitt also hired promoters and even some local criminals for marketing purposes. He worked deals with promoters, including one known as Cool Runnin', who had the ear of thousands of black Atlanta-area residents. Cool Runnin' tried to pressure Bitt for a piece of Platinum, as he wanted more than just a cut of the cover charges. Bitt quickly nipped the request in the bud by telling him he should be happy with the arrangement to split the cover on the agreed-upon nights, or he could expect a stray bullet in his head. Cool Runnin' quit asking for a share of ownership in Platinum after that clarification was made.

Often referring to Platinum as Felon Heaven, Bitt drew the rough crowds one would have expected considering his close association with the BMF. He even hired some technically savvy people to attend major black entertainment events at Phillips Arena and other venues and steal the cell numbers of the attendees with a machine. In this manner, messages promoting the club were blasted via texts to potential black customers. Bitt's work life was now stabilized, as he worked at Peaches in the evening till midnight before going to Platinum, his first love.

During that time, Preston Bolton was running for sheriff in Forsyth County, a northern bedroom community of Atlanta. He approached Bitt and Ireland, asking for money to support his campaign. A Forsyth County deputy in Cumming, Bolton promised Bitt that he and Ireland could have the run of the county if he won the election. He even offered to let them eliminate people without concern of any serious investigations. Bitt and Ireland gave Bolton $10,000 for his election fund and even gave him a job so they had an excuse to funnel cash to him.

Although Bolton promised Bitt he could do anything in Forsyth County, he crossed Bitt by making advances toward his ex-wife Rhonda. He tried to impress her by telling her he was going to arrest Bitt and Ireland after he was elected. Unfortunately for Bolton, she told Bitt of this boast, and he decided to set Bolton up to be arrested. Bitt taped conversations with Bolton in which he specifically promised to allow Bitt to kill anyone he wanted and to dump bodies in Forsyth County. Raymond Montington, a Gainesville FBI agent, worked with Bitt and arrested Bolton in 2004 based primarily on the tapes supplied by Bitt.

Bitt owned four houses by that time, including a large house in Alpharetta, Georgia, and a farm in Newnan, Georgia, south of Atlanta. He also owned a condominium in Panama City, Florida, but never visited it. He paid cash for most of his residences, and he later would sell the farm and buy a house in Wynfield, an affluent addition in Cumming, Georgia. Including another large house in the exclusive Oakmont subdivision in Cumming, Bitt paid a total of $26,000 a month in mortgage payments, pool upkeep, and other overhead expenses. His third wife, Rhonda, lived in the Wynfield home off and on between extended trips to pursue her dream of becoming a singer and actress. Rhonda ran Bitt's limousine service when she was in town. He usually ran two to three cars, keeping the operation small and headache free. Bitt was a silent owner in the business, and it generated approximately $200,000 in annual revenues, with about a 50 percent profit margin. He bought a new 120 limo every few years. During the years he provided female companionship out of Dolls Downtown in Augusta during the Masters Golf Tournament, he purchased a new limousine in early April a few times. He was able to pay off the new vehicle with part of his earnings during the weeklong tournament event.

Bitt still loved the uncertainty and volatility of his fast-paced lifestyle as a nightclub entrepreneur. He and Ireland were usually in step with the local authorities but not always. In the early 2000s, the FBI asked for a meeting with Bitt and Ireland. They asked Ireland if they could talk to him and Bitt at Ireland's mansion in Roswell. In a show of force, twenty-five agents showed up in four vans for the meeting, including Raymond Montington, an FBI agent who had already recommended arresting Bitt and Ireland on racketeering charges. Montington announced that they were preparing to arrest both of them for allowing prostitution and the sale of drugs at Peaches. Bitt vigorously denied these charges and suspected that the threat to indict them was a bluff. They ordered Ireland to turn over all of his guns to them, and it took an hour and a half to receive and record them. He had everything from hand guns to rifles to assault weapons. Although the feds didn't check Ireland's car, he typically carried as many as twelve guns at a time in it.

Bitt reminded Ireland more than once not to say anything until their attorney was present. Within an hour of the invasion, Attorney Louis Levenson showed up to negotiate with the FBI on behalf of Ireland and Bitt. Eventually, the feds presented a wish list of what they wanted in order to save Bitt and Ireland from arrest or to prevent a raid of Peaches. They demanded that Bitt and Ireland wear wires to gain incriminating information on the following individuals: Gold Club owner Arthur Dennison; Gambino family crime lord John A. Gotti Jr.; Gold Club owner, drug dealer, and limousine mogul Mitchell LeFlore; three later-to-be-named crooked Atlanta police officers; certain members of the Atlanta Russian mob; and others.

They kept Bitt and Ireland in Ireland's house for almost twenty-four hours. Bitt was certain they didn't have enough to charge them. The feds took Ireland to Peaches while Bitt stayed behind. They showed Ireland several cars and agents who were purportedly ready to raid his club. He caved in and agreed to cooperate, so they took him home, where Bitt and their attorney were waiting. Bitt had decided to cooperate with respect to some of the targets on the list but not all of them. He was steadfast in his refusal to become involved in any sting operation or wear a wire involving the Russian mob or other organized-crime figures, such as John A. Gotti Jr. and Dennison. Bitt was turned loose, and he called Atlanta Police Department officer Garrett Royal, whom he considered a friend. Bitt strongly advised Royal to stay away from Peaches and said he should give the same advice to his law enforcement colleagues. He told Royal that the feds were after him and other cops. He further repeated some of the things he had heard that indicated the feds had him and his colleagues on audio and video. However, Bitt was clear to Royal that he was of the opinion the feds didn't have enough to charge him at the time. Royal thanked Bitt and agreed to stay away.

A couple weeks later, the FBI was still negotiating with Levenson, Bitt, and Ireland. They asked Bitt why they were getting no more video of the cops outside Peaches. Bitt told him he had warned them to stay away from the club. The agents were furious and threatened to bring charges against him. Bitt stood his ground and told them to go ahead, figuring they wanted him to help them too badly to act on their threat. He retorted that they had no formal agreement yet, and he considered the cops to be friends. Amazingly, Royal showed up at Peaches again about six months later. Bitt was flabbergasted and asked him what he was doing in the club. It turned out that Royal missed the sex with the dancers too much to stay home. He had married into to an influential family in Cumming. The feds had the club wired and under camera surveillance.

Bitt reinstated payments to Royal of $500 a week, which were now being provided by the FBI. During the next several months, he gave Royal several thousand dollars of federal funds for his family vacations. Several other local police officers were regulars at Peaches and also on Bitt's payroll, now partially funded by taxpayers. Peaches enjoyed freedom from being hassled by the local police as a result of the payments to several officers. Eventually, Royal was arrested and pleaded guilty to avoid a trial. He served time and was released; his career in law enforcement was over. He later worked in the insurance industry but held no grudge against Bitt. Royal's wife left him, and he began refereeing Atlanta-area youth basketball games. A former Division I basketball player at Georgetown, he and Bitt later ran into each other at a local youth sports facility. He told Bitt he would have done the same thing if he had been in his shoes. Bitt was to do more work for the FBI, including helping put away a bomb maker who was on the FBI's watch list.

CHAPTER 23

By 2003, Bitt was living on his forty-acre "gentleman's farm" in Newnan, Georgia. He attended church services at First Baptist Church of Cumming about once a month or so, since it was about a hundred-mile round trip. He felt guilty about his lavish lifestyle but saw no way out of it. Furthermore, he still enjoyed it, even though he knew it was wrong. He scaled back a little on his workload and took a day or two off once in a while. One thing he never missed was his weekly trip for a couple of hours to view competing nightclubs. The purpose was to keep his reputation and name known to the dancers at the other clubs with the idea in mind that he might hire them at some point in the future. This consistent routine worked wonders in that he always had dancers wanting to work for him.

Bitt ran Platinum 21 until 2010. He preferred managing it

over Peaches because it was more on the edge, due in part to its popularity with the BMF. There were frequent gun battles in Platinum's parking lot, and eight fatalities occurred in one year alone. Instead of dreading parking lot shootings, Bitt relished them. Many times, when a shooting broke out in the parking lot, bystanders stampeded their way into the club to escape the flying bullets. They risked being run down by Bitt, who was charging in the opposite direction toward the action. A self-described psycho, Bitt was drawn to these battles. Since he didn't carry a weapon, his initial move was typically to overpower and disarm one of the gunmen to secure a piece.

Cedartown, Georgia, was a small town about sixty miles west of Atlanta. It also happened to be the hometown of Bitt's third wife, Rhonda Woodard. He purchased a twenty-acre property near Cedartown from Rhonda's parents. It had a twenty-thousand-square-foot building on the land that included living quarters but was not being used. Bitt paid $250,000 for the property and turned the building into a Mexican nightclub for Rhonda to operate. Rhonda was the owner of record. He named it Pebbles, which was also Rhonda's dancing moniker. As were most of Bitt's ventures, the club was a success, at least initially. The Mexican clientele embraced the club and made it successful. Rhonda knew what would be successful, and she correctly predicted that many husbands and wives would attend together. Bitt remodeled the building and added a side room to the main area for exotic dancers, which was accessible after paying a second cover charge of twenty-five dollars. Typically, the Mexican patrons put on their best clothes and packed three to four hundred into the club, paying an entry cover charge of twenty-five dollars each. The door charges alone generated $10,000 to $15,000 a week, and alcohol sales added another $10,000 to $15,000. In less than four months, the club had paid for itself and was turning a tidy profit.

Rhonda prepared Bitt for what she knew would be an all-too-common occurrence: an evening-ending lively fight. Two groups of combatants, usually consisting of ten to twelve family members, relatives, and friends, would square off in the parking lot of Pebbles around closing time. There were no weapons, and the contests were usually short in duration, with one side declaring itself the winners, and everyone went home. Never one to be concerned about having too much to handle, Bitt looked in on Pebbles a couple of Saturday nights a month since he had Peaches and Platinum 21 running relatively smoothly. Pebbles was open on Saturday nights only.

The popularity of Pebbles grew among the Hispanic community, and soon crowds of four to five hundred were jamming into the establishment. Additionally, up to a thousand began congregating on some nights in the parking lot to party. This concerned Bitt, and he began charging for parking, further boosting the club revenues. However, the club's clientele began to change, and everyone who spoke Spanish began attending, including Peruvians, Haitians, Jamaicans, Cubans, and other ethnicities. This mixture of cultures, unfortunately, led to violence between the different factions, and things became ugly quickly. There was a shooting in the parking lot that led to a fatality. The Georgia Bureau of Investigation's Douglas Donlan had an informant working for him in the area, and he contacted Bitt shortly after the parking-lot death. Bitt had previously told Donlan that he had acquired Pebbles. Donlan told Bitt that his confidential informer had told him there was recently a "crazy unarmed man in an orange sports coat" standing between two Hispanic gangs in the Pebbles parking lot, trying to keep them from shooting each other. Donlan, figuring the man had been Bitt, had called to check how he was doing.

From Nightlife to Eternal Life

Pebbles went downhill after the shooting. Rhonda and her brothers tried to draw a different clientele to the club, but they closed it about a year after it opened. This was in stark contrast to Platinum 21, where shootings were much more common. A striking difference between the short-lived Pebbles and Platinum 21 was that shootings seemed to bolster Platinum's popularity. Its patrons didn't want to miss anything, and the door counts grew in the days following a gunfight.

Bitt was overextended in terms of his jobs and all of the properties he owned. He still relieved drug dealers of their cash whenever he needed some funds. These events usually occurred two to three times a year. These extracurricular activities allowed for some major projects, such as the remodeling of Platinum 21, which cost nearly $250,000. As always, he never made it a secret that he was the one who robbed the various drug dealers and pushers. Despite his lack of concern about his victims knowing who he was, he seldom faced any attempted retribution.

One notable exception took place while he was living in the Oakmont home in Cumming. He received word via the grapevine that a drug crew he had robbed was coming after him. He sent his family out of town and sat by his pool for a few days with his good friend and employee Larry Reed. Some of the Platinum 21 dancers came to his house to cook and entertain Bitt, Reed, and another friend. Bitt had various types of guns in different places around the pool. After about four days of sitting outside and watching the street, they noticed a black Navigator trimmed in gold with spinners on its wheels coming down the main road toward the house. In his bathing suit and carrying an AR-15, he ran down the street right at the approaching car. The four men in the vehicle quickly turned around and left the neighborhood.

A few weeks later, Bitt was in Peaches, and a customer told him that one of the four guys who'd been in the Navigator was in the club. After the individual was pointed out to him, Bitt went up to him, took him to the ground, and disarmed him. Bitt then took the gun and pistol-whipped him. Following this, Bitt racked a bullet into the chamber, put the gun in the would-be assassin's hand, and pressed it against his own head. He then told him to go ahead and kill him if he was man enough and was willing to do thirty years for murder. This was another example of Bitt's fearlessness and reckless disregard for his own safety. Years later, he would come to realize that for whatever reason, God was protecting him. He faced countless dangerous situations and was never seriously injured.

Reed found Bitt to be someone who could take a nightclub over and manage it to the next level financially, as Bitt was constantly three or four steps ahead of everyone around him and was very intelligent. Working for him at Platinum and Peaches, he knew Bitt as someone who would make money for partners and associates in the club industry while demanding that they deal honestly with him or face the consequences. He was amazed at Bitt's smooth way with customers and the fact that he could slap them around and then influence them to stay longer and spend more money.

CHAPTER 24

Money was flowing into Bitt's hands and leaving them almost as quickly. He earned a salary from Ireland but continued to make more on tips. Bitt and Ireland bought, bartered, and sold all types of goods. They traded in flat-screen TVs, appliances, clothes, diamonds, meat, and all types of consumer goods. Not concerned about the source of the goods purchased, they typically sold items at big discounts. Plasma TVs were $10,000 when they first came out, but Bitt acquired some and sold them at half price. Most of his hustles originated with customers in Peaches or Platinum 21. He also dabbled with acquiring other nightclubs, buying one once in a while in someone else's name.

However, he had visions of going straight when he lived at the farm in Newnan County. He began selling truckloads of goods he and Ireland acquired from legitimate sources, such as Costco.

He even donated items to Crossroads, a local Baptist church. He rented a warehouse to hold all of the goods he was acquiring to sell to local customers. Bitt spread the word that he had opened, essentially, a flea market. The first time he had a "yard sale," he made $5,000 in profits. He believed he had found a niche to make clean money and began holding events on a weekly basis. He also held monthly auctions at his warehouse.

He drew the attention of the local Newnan law enforcement community, who feared Bitt was going to bring some form of the adult entertainment industry into their fair town. They took advantage of a mistake Bitt made when he became angry at a contractor. He hired a local builder and remodeler to do some custom brick work and other improvements at his farm home to the tune of about $40,000. The Caucasian Newnan contractor hired by Bitt made some critical comments about his own Brazilian workers. He also made the big mistake of letting Bitt hear him say he hoped the second floor of the house would cave in and kill Bitt's two "half-breed children," referring to Kalie and Calie. This irritated Bitt to no end. He liked the small-statured Brazilian laborers, whom he found to be good guys and hard workers. Needless to say, no one with any sense of self-preservation criticized Bitt's children. Following his sense of justice, he lured the offensive-mouthed contractor into his barn and beat some sense into him. Losing a few of his teeth and requiring a brief stay in a local hospital, the contractor filed a complaint with the police.

While Bitt was working in Atlanta a few days later, local law enforcement officers obtained a warrant and raided the farm. They conducted a search for an alleged underground meth lab, guns, and drugs. They found no lab or any drugs. Fortunately for Bitt, they didn't find a stash of illegal guns hidden in a tractor trailer truck near his barn. The search turned up little besides about $5,000 in cash and some DVDs of *The Godfather* and other gangster movies. They spread out the money and the DVD covers and photographed them as part of an indictment. Bitt had to cut a plea deal to avoid being called before the grand jury. He agreed to leave Newnan and not return. As a result, his six-month attempt to go clean ended. He was told by local cops that his reputation had preceded him, and the local authorities feared he would try to skirt around the local statutes and open a sex club. His actual desire was to rent and eventually buy the warehouse in which he was running the occasional auctions and weekly yard sales. He envisioned putting in a car lot and even a restaurant. He was disappointed because he wanted to go straight. Bitt hung on to his ranch for several years and leased it to friends at various times, including Larry Reed.

He also rented the farm to Jason Jonesboro, whom Bitt met when he hung out at Peaches. Jonesboro and a friend began coming into the club and throwing around fifty- and hundred-dollar bills. Recognizing a mark when he saw one, Bitt identified Jonesboro as someone from whom he could take some money at some point. Unfortunately, Jonesboro's friend began having a relationship with one of club owner Bob Ireland's girlfriends, a Bulgarian bartender at Peaches. Jonesboro also began dating one of the other club employees, also a Bulgarian, but one night, he and his buddy went too far. As they were leaving with their dates, they crumpled up some large bills and threw them at Ireland's feet when they walked out Platinum's door. Jonesboro and his friend had stolen more than a million dollars from a pot grower and dealer. They also had taken some strands and seeds with the idea of starting a grow house.

Jonesboro, with a $500,000 stash, rented Bitt's farm for $2,600 a month. He stayed about ten months but fell behind in his rent payments, as he wasted his money in Peaches and a couple of other clubs. When he was several months behind in rent payments, Jonesboro transferred the registration papers for his Mercedes over to Bitt to settle his debt. It appeared that Bitt came out ahead. He was happy to accept the new car for the back rent, as it was worth more than $50,000. Unfortunately, Bitt's ex-wife Rhonda Woodard dropped into Peaches as the transaction was being consummated. She fell in love with the Mercedes and begged Bitt to let her drive it. He reluctantly agreed, and she promised to return it later in the day. About twenty-four hours later, Bitt learned that Rhonda had wrecked the car and seriously injured a female passenger. The car was legally Bitt's but now was worthless.

Shortly after the car was ruined, Bitt was visiting with an ATF undercover agent at Peaches. He introduced the agent to Jonesboro. Jonesboro swapped cell numbers with the agent, who eventually asked Jonesboro if he could supply guns to sell to Iranian and Pakistani insurgents. Falling hook, line, and sinker for the ATF sting, Jonesboro secured some guns for the ATF agent and also bragged that he knew how to make roadside bombs for the right price. Jonesboro was living at Bitt's Newnan farm when he put the noose around his own neck by providing guns and promises of homemade bombs to the ATF. Jonesboro depleted all of his funds from dealing grass, and the ATF feared he might become more radical and make a bomb for a terrorist cell. After he was arrested, the ATF discovered that Jonesboro was an escaped federal prisoner.

The ATF agent who reeled in Jonesboro was on good terms with Bitt and informed Bitt that the DEA and ATF suspected him of providing transportation to a jewel-theft team operating in the Southeast, which was patently untrue. Later, Bitt visited in Peaches with Jed Stauffer, the South Florida pimp who'd previously tried to hire him to manage a string of Florida nightclubs. He asked probing questions of Bitt in connection to the jewelry heists, and Bitt correctly surmised that Stauffer was wearing a wire. He gave him nothing incriminating or anything even suggesting he might have knowledge of the string of jewelry thefts, and in fact, he didn't know anything about them.

Later, the DEA made another move to rope in Bitt in the form of a target letter. Not a summons or an indictment, the communication asked Bitt to come in to talk with them about the string of jewelry robberies. Bitt engaged the services of his attorney, Louis Levenson. The two met with the DEA. Nothing came of the interview, as Bitt truly had nothing to tell them. Jonesboro

Jim Henninger

was later tried in federal court. Bitt and Larry Reed testified against him. He was found guilty and sentenced to a prison term. Bitt didn't get in trouble, although Jonesboro was arrested on his farm. The property was then officially owned by his mother, but he continued to rent out the property to acquaintances.

CHAPTER 25

In 2004, Bitt made another attempt to enter into a legitimate industry: the used-car business. This time, Bitt was on the wrong end of a con. He sold the Newnan farm to a used-car dealer, Colby Herbert. He paid Bitt more than the market value and threw in a Florida condominium as part of the payment. Bitt then gave his new partner $200,000 for improvements on Colby's car lot. There were almost two hundred cars on the lot, but unbeknownst to Bitt, Herbert only owned six of them. After giving him the money to put into the business, Bitt went to the lot, and almost all of the cars had been removed. He learned that Herbert used the money he gave him to pay off personal and business debts. Herbert then had the audacity to ask him for another $200,000. Bitt refused his request. Bitt told him he would take him out back to give him what he deserved if he didn't leave immediately. Herbert departed, and Bitt never saw him again, deciding that the money lost was not worth the trouble he would encounter to pursue it. He regretted being scammed, but over the years, his gains far outweighed his losses.

In 2005, Bitt became involved in the local boxing circuit in Atlanta as an owner and sponsor. Boxing touched Bitt's heart. It also gave him a feel of legitimacy, but his past kept rearing its ugly head and short-circuiting his efforts to become involved in an above-board livelihood. The sport of boxing had always interested Bitt, and he was proud of the fact that his father had sparred twice with former heavyweight champion Joe Louis during his time of service in the US Army. Thus, entering into the world of boxing allowed Bitt to honor his father's memory. One of Bitt's club security employees, Noie Reyes, knew Jorge "Babyface" Lacierva, who was, at various times, a super bantamweight, a bantamweight, and a featherweight. Bitt immediately liked Lacierva, who was a sharp dresser, was well spoken, and made a nice impression on others. Bitt hired him as a part-time security associate at Platinum, and he was well liked by the other employees. Lacierva lost two fights early in his career in Mexico but had already been in some minor classification title fights for up-and-comers when Bitt befriended him. Lacierva's father paved the way for him to take up boxing, as he was a well-known veteran pugilist in Mexican fighting circles.

Bitt began attending boxing matches in Atlanta, often purchasing seats for himself, Platinum customers, and friends. Club dancers even served as ring card girls, marching around the boxing ring between rounds and holding up placards announcing the upcoming round number. Ever the promoter for Peaches and Platinum, Bitt donated ring card girls for the opportunity to allow one of his club's deejays to announce the fight, plug Peaches and Platinum, and have his dancers pass out flyers to patrons.

Lacierva came to Bitt as an unknown but eager boxer with great potential. He fought in the feature matches at different local venues, such as the Gwinnett Civic Center, under Bitt's control. In the daytime, the young boxer worked out, and in the evenings, he was a bouncer for Bitt at Platinum. He earned $400 to $500 a week for working four to five hours a day. He was also an asset in that his diminutive size and solid punching power came in handy with rowdy club customers. He was married with two young children and even came to see Bitt's son play youth football.

Prior to one of his fights, Lacierva invited Bitt's son to

accompany him to his training venue in Austin, Texas. The younger Thrower stayed and worked out for a couple of weeks. He came home in good shape, but more importantly, he'd formed a lifelong friendship with the personable boxer. Bitt didn't take any promoter's or manager's fees from Lacierva's purses at first in an attempt to get him in better personal financial shape and to gain his trust and loyalty. The industry norm was for a manager to take a percentage of the money earned for each fight. Bitt worked hard for Lacierva, as he did in whatever venture he undertook. In a short time, he lined up bouts for his 126-pound class boxer in Las Vegas at Caesar's Foxes, MGM, and Mandalay Bay. He was on the undercard one time in front of a Bernard Hopkins title fight. He also fought in Hidalgo, Texas, one of the hotbeds of Mexican American boxing.

Lacierva's big opportunity came when Bitt landed him an undercard bout prior to a championship fight involving World Boxing Council (WBC) champion Israel Vazquez. Lacierva's opponent was Celestino Caballero, a Panamanian fighter who held the International Boxing Federation (IBF) and WBC titles. Caballero won in a unanimous decision in Dodge Arena in Hidalgo. Lacierva came out strong and did well in the first eight rounds. The odds were 14–1 against Lacierva, and most observers thought he beat Caballero, but the judges apparently didn't see it that way. Bitt didn't attend, as he had pressing matters to attend to in Atlanta, but he became convinced that Lacierva lost the decision because the venue, Dodge Arena, would have gone bankrupt if Caballero had lost the fight and bets against him had to be honored.

Instead of being disappointed, Bitt grew excited at the prospect of taking Lacierva to the top of his profession. He felt his boxer could win some big-time bouts and avoid subjective judging in the future. He even picked up some more boxers as he began to assimilate his own stable of fighters. Again, he harbored hopes of getting into a legitimate line of business, but it wasn't meant to be. He formed a relationship with a smaller boxing organization, CAM, which had vacancies in many of its weight classifications. CAM's main requirement, as was normal with many boxing organizations, was that promoters prove they had money and were willing to part with it. Bitt had the cash and started arranging for local fights to further groom Lacierva, whom he guided to a top-ten ranking. He ran across another young boxer, Rummel "Tank" Rene, who tired of being in Don King's group of fighters. He was undefeated when he started fighting under Bitt's direction in the Atlanta area. The relationship with Rene was short-lived and tumultuous. On one occasion, Rene brought a thug with him into Platinum, and they sought out Bitt. They accused him of taking the money Rene earned from boxing. Bitt asked him what money he was talking about since he took none of the fighter's modest purses and, in fact, paid him a salary, fed him, and bought him clothes. The ex-con threatened Bitt and informed him that he was now Rene's manager. Never one to back down from a challenge, Bitt told the would-be manager that he had a proposition for him. Bitt said that unless he changed his tune, neither the thug nor Rene would leave the club in the next hour without sporting two broken hands with every bone and every finger fractured. Such injuries to a boxer were the kiss of death and career ending. The two left the club without incident. That discussion ended Bitt's relationship with Rene.

Bitt put a lot of money into the sport of boxing as a sponsor, manager, and promoter. He got excited when he picked up a promising heavyweight, Cedric Boswell, who hadn't fought for three years but had a record of 21–1. He had watched a fight card involving Lacierva that was held at the Rialto. Bitt organized the event, and it was a success, although it cost him a lot of money. However, he met Boswell, who introduced himself to Bitt at the affair. Not long afterward, Bitt picked up Boswell and paid him $5,000 a month to train. He was also allowed to keep all of his purses. That was a sweet deal for Boswell, but Bitt wanted to keep him happy. With all of the other expenses, including a hyperbolic chamber, he arranged for an undercard championship bout for Boswell, who was known as the Bos. In 2007 and 2008, Boswell fought six times under Bitt's direction and quickly moved up in the rankings. Boswell was closing in on a big payday as he rose to a number-four ranking in the WBA. Bitt was in discussions for a Las Vegas bout at the MGM for Boswell, who won the IBF North American and USBA heavyweight titles by beating Roman Greenberg in Atlanta in 2008. Bitt spent more than $100,000 putting together the fights for the IBF and USAB titles. The cost included fees for sanctioning by the governing bodies and other expenses, including hotel rooms and meals for officials and other dignitaries.

During his few years in the fight game, Bitt spent more than $400,000 and made a return of only $150,000 in ticket sales and postfight parties at Platinum. However, he came close to closing a WBC heavyweight championship fight event that would have landed him $1 million to $2 million and plenty of collateral financial gains. He envisioned becoming a multimillionaire wheeling and dealing with Boswell, Lacierva, or both of them. Once he reached the big time, the monetary success would have been assured. About half of the funds Bitt needed for his boxing hobby were secured from relieving drug dealers of their cash holdings, as he had done on occasion in the past. One of the many expenses Bitt faced in the boxing industry was paying off boxing officials. One IBF official came to Atlanta and held discussions with Bitt. The official informed him that his fighter, Boswell, had a chance to move up in the rankings and agreed to move Boswell into the top ten of the IBF rankings for $10,000. Bitt paid the money and later coughed up another $20,000 following the Greenberg fight for a number-four ranking. In addition, free nights at Platinum for the officials cost Bitt thousands of dollars in drinks, food, and girls. Eventually, Bitt was told that a number-two ranking, which would lead to a shot at the IBF championship, would cost him $100,000. He never was able to make such an arrangement, because his legal problems soon derailed his boxing activities and everything else in his life.

Unfortunately, in 2008, Bitt hit a major roadblock. He was indicted in Atlanta for arson and would eventually face a three-year prison term. After splitting with Bitt, Boswell fought for the WBA World Heavyweight Title in 2011 against Alexander Povetkin but was knocked out. He never stepped into the ring again and finished his career at 34–2. Interestingly, both Boswell and Lacierva would later serve some jail time. Boswell was arrested on drug charges, and Lacierva, who never became a US citizen, was charged with firing a gun during a rampage in his own home. His wife had an affair with someone, and he caught them in the bedroom in a compromising position. He fired some bullets into the walls and ceilings but didn't hit his wife or her lover. Lacierva was later deported to Mexico after being charged in the shooting. Boswell served time during much of the same period in which Bitt was soon to be incarcerated.

CHAPTER 26

Despite his reluctance to give up his nightclub life and occasional undercover assignments, Bitt was slowly drawing closer to the Lord. Although his attempts to get into legitimate businesses were not coming to fruition, he wasn't ready to give up. Beginning in the late 1990s, he started attending First Baptist Church of Cumming on a regular basis, taking his son and his twin daughters with him. He formed some relationships with a few members, specifically Larry Townsend, a country gentleman approaching eighty years old. Townsend noticed a big, tough-looking guy coming to church most Sundays and sitting in the back row. Townsend sang in the choir and noticed that the large man got up and practically ran out of the services with his kids in tow every Sunday he attended. One day Townsend chased Bitt down in the lobby as he was heading out the door. He called out to him, "Hey, big guy. Can I talk to you a minute?"

Bitt was not happy, as his mind raced with possibilities of what the gruff old man might want from him. He conjured up thoughts that Townsend might be someone he had run across in a club or elsewhere. He thought to himself, *Lord, please don't put me in a position where I'm in a confrontation in your house.* Wearing an Armani suit, a Rolex watch, and $1,500 shoes, Bitt reluctantly turned around and asked him, "What can I do for you, sir?" Townsend shook his hand and told him that he had noticed him in the back row, singing the hymns. He added that he could see he knew all of words to the different songs without referring to a hymnal. He then told Bitt he was impressed with his familiarity with the songs and was glad he was attending the services.

Bitt was taken aback by this friendly gesture from someone he didn't know. It nearly brought tears to his eyes, and he knew that God's hand was involved in this seemingly random greeting. This simple act of kindness by Townsend touched Bitt's heart, and he eventually formed a close relationship with Townsend, who'd also been a rough-and-tumble character in years past. Bitt also came to know the pastor and the youth minister. He was surprised to find out that they accepted him, although they didn't condone his lifestyle. Bitt didn't hide the details of his life, and both church staff members encouraged Bitt to get out of the strip clubs and do something else for a living. Bitt knew he needed to change, but he couldn't quite bring himself to break off from his boss, Bob Ireland; Peaches; Platinum; and occasionally robbing drug dealers. He thought his financial setbacks in boxing, a sports bar, a used-car lot, and earlier ventures were the devil messing with him and not allowing him to change his life and get closer to God. He hadn't grasped the concept of turning his life completely over to Jesus and loving others. He later would find out that it was going to take a mind-rattling blow to bring him out of his life of chasing the almighty dollar and hustling others. He had to slow down somehow, and his time for change was coming, just not how he envisioned it. Ironically, Bitt was going to find peace and contentment in 2010, shortly after he began to serve a thirty-two-month sentence in the federal prison system. He was about to take himself off of the streets by burning down a competing nightclub to put it out of business.

A club catering to white clientele, Onyx, opened its doors just down the street from Platinum. It soon became a thorn in Bitt's

From Nightlife to Eternal Life

side. Jack Galardi, the owner of other local nightspots as well as clubs in Las Vegas and elsewhere, opened the new ten-thousand-square-foot facility in 2006. At first, there was no tension, as Platinum's black customers continued to patronize Bitt's business as usual. However, that was about to change. Jermaine Dupri decided to rent the Onyx and hold a party. Dupri, a record producer, song writer, and rapper, owned and operated the So So Def record company. Street rumors had it that Dupri paid between $50,000 and $100,000 to rent the Onyx for what turned out to be a huge one-night party. It was a hip-hop and rap extravaganza and drew up to a thousand attendees. Dupri invited black rap stars from across the country, and Galardi quickly realized he could turn a tidy profit if he catered to the black rap lovers in Atlanta. A second event soon followed in the form of a free weekend party headlined by hip-hop artist Luke Skywalker from Miami, Florida, and including notable rappers, such as Jeezy. Free food and drinks were provided, and the turnout was unprecedented in a black Atlanta nightclub. Platinum couldn't compete with that type of event, as it was too small to hold crowds of the size the Onyx was drawing.

The Onyx began to raid Platinum of their best dancers, but

more importantly, Platinum's revenue began to diminish. The weekly receipts dropped from $70,000 to $80,000 down to less than $40,000. Bitt warned his three managers that the drop in revenues meant their perks, bonuses, and tips would go away. Bitt asked the managers to hit the streets to find new dancers and take their current ones to events to drum up business. He gave them two weeks to find a way to make more money before their incomes were affected. The Platinum general manager, Boyd Smith, and the rest of the management crew came up with an idea and presented it to Bitt: blow up Onyx. One of Smith's managerial hires, Sandeo Dyson, was also a key player. A US Army Ranger stationed in Dahlonega, Georgia, Dyson had a group of fellow soldiers already working with him in security at Platinum. Bitt told the group to slow down and go easy. As a result, they tried other avenues to undermine Onyx. One night, a Platinum security employee went to Onyx and started a fight by breaking a champagne bottle over a customer's head. A melee ensued, and shots were fired. Patrons cleared out immediately, and many of them went down the street to Platinum. As a result, Bitt's club enjoyed a profitable evening. Another evening, Bitt's crew drove to Onyx and sprayed the club with automatic gunfire, dispersing the crowd and again boosting Platinum's business for the evening.

These disruptions continued as the Platinum employees tried several ways to give Onyx a bad name. On one occasion, they put a large number of roaches in Onyx to try to repulse its customers. These types of attempts went on for a few months until Dyson called Bitt at home in the early overnight hours of January 2, 2007, despite the rule that Bitt was never to be called at home. Bitt feared that his phone was tapped, and it turned out that it was. Dyson told Bitt that there was currently a five-alarm fire on Piedmont Road. Dyson had torched the Onyx by hiding in the club when it closed and starting an inferno. Initially, Platinum prospered, as all of its lost customers returned, and the money began flowing once again. The change occurred overnight with the demise of the Onyx. However, the fire would soon backfire on Bitt, Smith, and Dyson. Bitt's knowledge of the plan to burn the Onyx would lead to his downfall despite the fact that he wasn't directly involved in setting the blaze. He would admit that he was guilty as sin, even though he wasn't at the scene of the crime. Fortunately, no one was hurt, as Dyson made sure the club was empty. Interestingly, there was never any retribution or contact from Galardi, who had to have strong suspicions about who set the fire.

Law enforcement and fire officials almost immediately declared the fire as arson. The owner of the Onyx was a well-known adult-industry mogul and organized-crime figure, which might have resulted in a less-than-expedient investigation. Bitt hoped that a lackluster look would be taken and that the investigation would eventually go dormant. However, that was not to be the case. He was certain the local police knew who benefited from the Onyx shutting down, namely him and his associates just down the street. Just as arrogant as ever, Bitt did not keep the event a secret. He confided in his attorney and some other close friends. This led to him being indicted in 2008. A major factor in Bitt's arrest for his role in the fire was his connection with Dyson and his army buddies. They made for an effective security team at Platinum, but they moved into bigger criminal activities after the fire incident. They were willing to do almost any strong-arm task for money and were often used by drug dealers and gangs in Atlanta. Bitt sometimes participated with them in their illegal schemes to pick up extra cash, but he worried they were becoming overconfident

From Nightlife to Eternal Life

and veering out of control. At the same time, Bitt still kept ripping off individual drug dealers to further supplement his income.

Bitt heard nothing about the investigation until the ATF contacted him at his home in 2008. They told him they had enough evidence to indict him for arson from information secured by wire taps. Bitt immediately figured out who had betrayed him, but he eventually forgave him and never sought to get even. The ATF asked Bitt to help them get the ever-escalating soldier gang off of the streets. Dyson's crew had graduated to kidnappings and other more serious offenses, including making people disappear. As part of a sting, Bitt introduced the soldiers, who trusted him, to a supposed drug dealer who was, in fact, an ATF agent. The agent told the soldiers he knew the location of a stash house used by a Mexican drug cartel, and he said it was full of product and cash. Bitt set up the soldiers by arranging a series of meetings between them and the ATF undercover agent. A raid of the fake drug house by the renegade soldiers was planned.

When the raid went down, the five soldiers and Bitt broke in to steal an expected ten to twenty kilos of cocaine and untold amounts of cash. Dyson, who was transferred to another base, was not present. In reality, the military group was about to meet ATF agents. As always, Bitt didn't bring a weapon with him, but the soldiers supplied him with an M-4 carbine. Of course, he never fired it. The group went to pick up what was supposed to be a stolen car in a storage unit in Roswell, Georgia, which was being supplied by the turncoat dealer. Bitt had a key to the unit, and in a prearranged signal, he yelled out, "Hey, the key won't work!" Immediately, ATF agents rushed onto the scene from the roofs of nearby units, parked vehicles, and other storage units. The soldiers surrendered without a shot being fired. Bitt was also taken down to the station but was released later in the evening. The soldiers began turning on each other right away. One of them called Dyson and told him the raid was a success. Dyson drove back to Georgia from Texas to pick up $20,000 in cash and five keys of cocaine and was arrested. Smith was arrested later for his role in the arson, as Dyson and Bitt flipped on him. Bitt and Dyson wanted to settle and avoid a trial, but Smith insisted on having his day in court. He was offered a one-year sentence in federal prison and refused it only to later be tried and sentenced to a five-year term in early 2010.

Bitt was back in Platinum and Peaches for about two years, managing the clubs before his incarceration began. He acted as if nothing were wrong, although rumors about his legal problems ran rampant. He briefly thought about taking his stash and his kids and running away, but he realized that a 320-pound man with two young daughters and a teenage son didn't make for an easy disappearance scenario. In the meantime, he was not under surveillance or restricted in any way. He attended First Baptist Church in Cumming, but he wasn't ready to give up his money-making activities. The district attorney told Bitt that he was going to recommend a twelve-month house arrest in recognition of his past undercover activities on behalf of the government and his cooperation in the sting. Bitt used a colleague of attorney Louis Levenson, Romine Alavi, to represent him. Alavi was a business associate of Ireland and a part-time interpreter and counsel for the DEA and other agencies. Alavi later served a prison term for violations caused by his addiction to prescription drugs. At one time, he was on the fast track to success and was in line for an appointment to an influential bench position in Atlanta metro's Cobb County.

CHAPTER 27

Bitt was living a life in two worlds by the time he was arrested for his role in the burning of the Onyx nightclub. He was managing Peaches and Platinum at night and attending First Baptist Church of Cumming on Sunday mornings. Oddly, he was comfortable in both environments. When FBC member Larry Townsend approached him after one of the services and welcomed him, the interaction turned Bitt around in his concept of the other members of the church. If a stand-up guy like Townsend accepted him, he might stand a chance of fitting in with the church and, just maybe, with God. However, he still felt the need to occasionally refill his till with confiscated money from drug dealers and pushers, as well as payments earned for occasional undercover assignments offered to him by federal agencies. With the previous open legal issue in Florida's Dade County still hanging over his head, Bitt felt obligated to accept nearly any request made of him by the CIA, DEA, ATF, or FBI. But the truth of it was that he enjoyed the thrill of working with black-ops agents.

The staff at FBC knew how Bitt made his living, at least the nightclub part of it. He continued to fight against God in that he tried to make himself a better person on his own terms and not those of the Holy Spirit. While he made some minimal progress, he refused to give in totally to God's will for his life. He failed in each attempt to legitimize himself from a business standpoint and rationalized these failures as reasons to continue making money in clubs and in other unsavory ways. He knew deep down that being a good person was not enough, even if he quit the club life and the robberies. Bitt's incarceration after being convicted of arson turned out to be the best thing that ever happened to him. He was at peace in prison and didn't worry about anything, as he finally adopted God's principles. He was in a den of sinners, where bad things occurred on a daily basis.

Bitt was not tried, as he and US Army Ranger Dyson pleaded guilty in hopes of receiving reduced sentences. Boyd Smith, Platinum general manager and the architect of the plan to torch the Onyx, refused to plead guilty and got his day in court. That was a big mistake. Both Bitt and Dyson were among several to testify against Smith. The whole trial and the publicity surrounding it were fodder for the news outlets in Atlanta and the Southeast. The combination of arson, renegade soldiers, nightclubs, girls, drugs, and big money made for interesting reading by the public. Neither Bitt nor Dyson wanted to testify against Smith, but they did so to keep alive their chances of being treated leniently at their sentencing arraignments. Smith was offered a one-year term in federal prison with the possibility of parole after ten months, and he should have taken it. He ended up serving a five-year term after a mountain of evidence proved he was guilty of planning and leading the criminal act.

Despite the publicity created by the trial, Bitt's value as an undercover informant and volunteer agent remained viable. He had garnered the trust of several agencies, who continued to utilize him for various roles in fighting drug and arms dealers. He was convinced that he would be given house arrest, but the judge had other ideas. Bitt had a cash stash and several passports for him and his family ready for a quick getaway, but he chose not to take that extreme measure. He didn't want his children to live on the run. The judge wanted to give Bitt the maximum sentence of five years, even though it was documented that he had been helpful in several undercover assignments. The court refused to give Bitt less than a three-year sentence, and he was devastated by the unwillingness to give him more consideration for his service to his country. A little-known fact is that Bitt was personally congratulated by Secretary of State Colin Powell for his off-the-books undercover efforts.

Prior to entering prison, Bitt worked out with weights to build himself up for his soon-to-come prison term. He wanted to build up his stamina so he could protect himself when he was placed in the general population of convicts. Before going to prison, Ireland sold Platinum to some Pakistanis from New York City. Ireland knew he wouldn't be able to control the black club, and both he and Bitt benefited from the sale, although Ireland was the legal owner. The new owners of Platinum weren't able to run it effectively and closed it down a short time later after paying $3 million for it. Before selling Platinum, Bitt, the same Pakistani group, and some other associates put a million dollars into a club purchased by Neal Skirvin, an Atlanta bookie. Skirvin came highly recommended by a friend of Bitt. The new business, the 24 Karat Gold Club, was remodeled with money provided by Bitt and his colleagues. For a short time, Bitt worked in Platinum, Peaches, and 24 Karat Gold Club at the same time. His relationship with Skirvin was based on a handshake, and Bitt never took any money from the operation of the club. However, when he went to prison, Skirvin turned on Bitt. The club went downhill without Bitt's management, and Skirvin's brothers, who worked at the club, were arrested for selling drugs onsite. Bitt used his influence with judges, state politicians, and law enforcement officials who frequented Peaches to reinstate the canceled liquor license in a few days instead of the customary ninety days. A ninety-day penalty would have been a death sentence for the ten-thousand-square-foot luxury club.

Skirvin began selling percentages of the club while Bitt was imprisoned, as he didn't know how to run it effectively. He made an enemy of Bitt for two reasons: he disrespected Bitt by not living up to verbal agreements concerning the club, and more importantly, he reneged on a personal agreement to give Bitt's family $5,000 a week while Bitt was in prison. He didn't keep his promise, and if not for Bitt's spiritual turnaround, Skirvin would likely have met a painful demise preceded by an attitude adjustment upon Bitt's release. Bitt stewed in his cell as he thought about all of the cash he'd put into Skirvin's club. To add insult to injury, Skirvin refused to pay a monthly bill for furniture financed for his club. Bitt had asked a friend, Moe Momey, to sign the purchase agreement for the furnishings but told him he wouldn't have to make the payments. When Skirvin refused to make the payments, Bitt's family was forced to honor the $1,800 monthly obligation to keep Moe out of hot water. Instead of a future gold mine, Bitt got nothing from Skirvin during his sentence or when he was released. His dream of retiring on his interest in the 24 Karat Gold Club was gone, along with a lot of his money.

Momey, who made his living in the valet parking industry, exemplified the opposite of Skirvin's actions. A Muslim, Momey used a little investment money from Bitt to help him build a small, successful business. He visited Bitt's family weekly while Bitt was in jail and gave them as much money as he could afford. He was consistent in his giving and his love for Bitt's children. Bitt had a special place in his heart for Moe, one of his most treasured friends. In the weeks before he reported to federal prison, Bitt assumed he was under surveillance by law enforcement agencies. Therefore, he kept busy working at Platinum and Peaches but didn't take any chances in getting involved in any extracurricular activities.

CHAPTER 28

On March 10, 2010, Bitt reported to Loretto Federal Prison. He voluntarily surrendered and later learned that this type of entry was a sign to other prisoners that you had money, because it meant you had the means to put up a bond before your incarceration. He was strip-searched upon entry, including comprehensive body-cavity probing. He was issued four uniforms and a few pairs of underwear, socks, and T-shirts. The only personal item allowed was a Bible, which Bitt brought in with him. He read it daily and wore the cover off of it. The change in his life was shocking in terms of the stoppage of his livelihood and being cut off from his family. He was initially placed in an open-air unit before being moved to a four-man cell. Bitt was concerned about his undercover work and the possibility that someone in the prison might be there because of him and hold a grudge against him. That didn't turn out to be a problem. He soon discovered there was an ample source of drugs, cigarettes, and food items if one had the money. The guards, poorly paid, were the brokers for illegal goods and successfully supplemented their incomes.

Prison food was poor in quality, but Bitt was more upset by the general lack of respect that the prison population had for each other. He found that many of the inmates didn't mind being there, and they strangely had no desire to take care of themselves from a hygiene standpoint. He found the weight room on the third day and began playing softball as much as possible. He again showed his aggression by pitching in slow-pitch games and charging the batters while the ball made its way to them. The same old Bitt was back playing softball. He quickly impressed his cellmates and others when he bench-pressed 275 pounds ten times after working his way up from fifteen repetitions at 225 and 250. Bitt usually lifted weights every second or third day after playing softball and tried to wear himself out before going to bed. He frequently did hundreds of repetitions with ninety-pound dumbbells.

He made friends with a Californian named Jim, who was serving a twenty-year term for his association with one of the Mexican drug cartels. He had made a lot of money and owned a home in San Diego. He also owned a beachfront residence in Mexico. He was a typical Southern Californian and introduced Bitt to Scotty, a rodeo tour cowboy who was jailed for selling meth to his friends and competitors. He had been only a casual meth user and hailed from North Carolina. He was serving a ten-year sentence. Bitt also met Barry, an attorney who'd had to leave a successful practice and formerly worked part-time as an expert on-air legal spokesman for the national TV networks. Bitt tried to surround himself with a better class of people than some of the dregs who were serving their time.

Bitt's first assignment was to a block of four- and six-man cells housing about a hundred inmates. For the most part, the inmates managed to get along, but that didn't last long for Bitt, as he ended up in the hole. He was cocky, and a few of the inmates knew him from one or more of the nightclubs he had managed. One large black inmate came up to Bitt one night after he finished making a phone call. Not knowing who he was, Bitt hung on to the phone in case he needed to wrap the phone cord around the giant's neck. It turned out that the man knew him from Platinum, and he told Bitt that his arrival had been news throughout the prison. He also said Bitt's reputation as a tough, violent guy had preceded his arrival at Loretta, and there were some Black Mafia Family inmates who knew or at least knew of him. He noticed that the different ethnic groups hung together in groups of blacks, Latinos, Guatemalans, Mexicans, Puerto Ricans, Cubans, Salvadorans, whites, and Colombians.

Bitt began working out by himself in the weight area, which was located in the yard. He did a lot of dumbbell work and would stay for two to three hours until he was exhausted. His routine was to lift and play softball as much as possible because that allowed him to stay outside longer. He also became an acquaintance with Tia, a former South Florida drug lord who had been associated with Pablo Escobar's organization. He was the prisoner representative who assigned the different jobs to the inmates. Bitt's assignment was to mop a section of a cell block under a stairwell by ten o'clock, before lights-out. Bitt's reputation led to his being propositioned to become involved in the cigarette trade, the drug trade, and the smuggled-cell-phone trade. He refused every opportunity, as he didn't want to do anything to possibly lengthen his sentence.

He did hook up with a group that cooked up meals from stolen food items and food purchased from guards and other inmates. They used a waste can and heated trash bags to prepare meals that were far tastier than the typical jail fare, and they sold the food to hungry inmates. However, Bitt experienced one bump in the road when he paid another inmate for six tomatoes and only received five. He quickly found the perpetrator and roughed him up. He often told his opponent he was killing him while squeezing his larynx and making him pass out. This event added to Bitt's reputation since he had administered punishment over a tomato. The next morning, Bitt woke up to find six tomatoes sitting by the door to his cell. He also smacked around another inmate who called him a rat for testifying against a defendant in federal court. Bitt left him in the stairwell that he was responsible for mopping.

Bitt got into a routine after a few months at Loretta. He had a hard time at night due to the changes in his thirty-year routine of working at night and sleeping during the day. He was trying to do his three years and not make friends or get into much in the way of extracurricular activities other than cooking and selling some meals. This approach rubbed some of his fellow prisoners the wrong way. Plus, he was arrogant and told others he was a stool pigeon who just wanted to do his time and get out. As always, he had no fear. He even drew the attention of the captain of the guards, a female, who couldn't believe Bitt was so direct in telling the population to leave him alone.

He tried to wear himself out during the day and then read his Bible and listened to the radio at lights-out, beginning at 10:00 p.m. He was lucky to drop off to sleep by one or two o'clock in the morning. He attended church services at the prison chapel on Sunday mornings, along with seventy-five to a hundred other inmates. Ministers from local churches delivered sermons, and the inmates formed a choir and sang hymns. Bitt experienced one unusual night during which he woke up wrapped up tightly in his sheet. He was amazed at how tight the sheet was, and he thought it resembled a funeral wrap like the ones he'd read about in the Bible. After he worked his way out of the sheet, his Christian cellmate at that time, who answered to Flight, told him, "God has released you from your bondage." Bitt then experienced a feeling of lightness and refreshment, and this peacefulness occurred periodically thereafter. He had no idea he was heading directly toward a spiritual awakening in the not-too-distant future.

He read his Bible diligently between card-playing sessions, exercise periods, and softball. He didn't run, but he walked a lot. One night, he and his buddies were cooking a big meal of chicken and all the fixings, utilizing the ballasts from the electric lights, trash liners, and ceramic trash cans. The process utilized steamers from the lights to heat water in the ceramic cans and cook items, such as rice and noodles to go with the chicken. The community TV for Bitt's block was just outside his cell. A Mexican biker who answered to Fats was interested in a Hispanic program scheduled to be on the set on a cook night in Bitt's cell. He had noticed that Fats was disrespectful to some of the other inmates, and Bitt told him he was a mean human being. He further told him that if he ever spoke to him in a disrespectful manner, he would take the TV off the wall and use it to decorate his skull. Trying to be diplomatic, a few nights later, he told Fats that he could use his assigned chair one night to watch his special show. It sat in the entrance to Bitt's cell. He further informed him that he would need to move for Bitt when he and his colleagues were carrying food in and out of the cell. Bitt and his buddies used cardboard boxes that twenty-four-packs of soft drinks came in as trays to deliver food to paying inmates. They lined the boxes with trash bags. Bitt had to ask Fats to move each time he entered or exited his cell to make deliveries and return.

The third time Bitt asked him to move, Fats spoke Spanish to his friends, and he used the word *puta*. Bitt returned a short time later and leaned over to speak to Fats. He reminded Fats that he had told him he would have to move frequently if he used the conveniently located chair. Bitt then asked Fats if he had the guts to tell him what he had said in Spanish a few minutes earlier to his companions. He also reminded him that he wasn't afraid of him, as everyone else in the prison was. Fats told Bitt the exact profanity-laced statement he had made to him when he was asked to move. Bitt's reaction was immediate. He leaned toward Fats and hit him with his elbow and forearm, knocking him out of his chair. He then pummeled him with his hands and feet. The other Hispanics flocked to the defense of Fats and went after Bitt, who threw them off while he kept attacking Fats. Of course, Scotty and Bitt's other friends came to his defense, and the melee spread throughout the block.

After a few minutes, everyone regrouped, and there was a lull in the fighting. By the last scheduled transition of the night, when the prisoners were allowed to go from one area to another, news of the incident had spread throughout the prison. Every Hispanic group agreed to come together to visit Bitt in his block. As a result, when the gates between the blocks opened about thirty minutes later, Bitt and his half dozen supporters were facing a crowd of more than a hundred Hispanics armed with shanks and combination locks in knotted white socks. Friends of Fats had already dragged him back to his cell to treat his injuries.

The unquestioned shot caller of the Hispanic population came to Bitt's cell. Bitt knew him from the weight-lifting room and the softball field. He told Bitt that he had figured it was him when he heard what had happened. Before negotiations got under way, the Hispanic point man told Bitt that retaliation was unavoidable, although he was sorry it had turned out to be him. At that moment, the guards came to the cell and asked Bitt to remove the beds and mattresses he and his group had used to barricade it. They then took him away and unceremoniously threw him in the hole, in solitary confinement. This seemingly negative outcome would turn out to be one of the best things to ever happen to Bitt.

CHAPTER 29

Bitt was questioned by prison officials, but he refused to talk. He was subjected to another body search, and his bloody clothes were taken from him and replaced with a clean uniform. His new home was a small cell about eight by eight feet with a miniature desk, toilet, bed, sheet, blanket, and pillow. There were no windows, and all of the furnishings were made of metal. He was moved to different cells in the hole every thirty days over the next six months. He started reading his Bible frequently and listening to Christian music and sermons on his radio.

It was a stark environment, but it became a place of peace for Bitt. He began to feel closer to God than he ever had before as he experienced solitude mixed with a comfortable feeling of spiritual peace. He started to work out for long hours each day by doing burpees, push-ups, and sit-ups and running in place. He checked into the hole weighing more than 320 pounds and trimmed down to about 290 pounds of lean muscle. He performed five hourly sessions of exercise routines, doing as many as a thousand push-ups a day. He was allowed to be outside for one hour a day in a small, fenced area, but the sky was visible. Bitt went outside every day regardless of the weather. The guards hated taking him, because they often had to venture in and out of the freezing weather. It was winter, and Bitt had a uniform made of thin material that didn't fend off the wind or the cold temperatures. He was chained at his legs and wrists while making the walk to the outside and back to the hole. He still insisted on going every day.

To attempt to break him of going outside, the guards began to leave him out in the cold for two to three hours instead of just one. But Bitt savored the experience, even though it brought with it the possibility of pneumonia. Incredibly, Bitt felt freedom for the first time in his life in the worst environment he had ever experienced. He exercised hard in the small pen and his cell every day. When he returned to the small cell, he stripped down to let his clothes dry out. He had a scratchy wool blanket to warm him up, but he still shivered for at least an hour. However, he didn't suffer. On the contrary, he felt good and more alive than ever. He knew that for the first time in his life, he was fully forgiven by Jesus Christ for all of the things he had done—and he forgave himself.

A few days later, one guard asked him, "Are we going to break you?"

Bitt replied, "No, sir, not as long as I can go outside. I've truly found the Lord." The guard was skeptical and told Bitt that everyone in prison found the Lord in heaven, but nobody wanted to go to heaven. Bitt loudly replied, "I'll tell you what. I'll go right now. Send me. Take me; I'm ready right now." He was sincere in his response.

The guard thought Bitt was losing his mind, because people went crazy in the hole due to the lack of personal contact. Many of them screamed at the top of their lungs at no one in particular. But Bitt was a new man, never to be the same and never to return to his former life. It was a miracle that few would have believed, and some never would believe, about Bitt Thrower.

Not long afterward, there was a riot in the general population, and the hole quickly became crowded. The small cells were meant for one man to be held in isolation, but the warden was forced to double up and place two men in many of them, creating situations where two criminals were on top of each other twenty-four hours a day. Some cells had three prisoners crammed in them until transfers could be arranged. Bitt was about to get a new cellmate, a Muslim named Lala. He didn't speak to Bitt for three days, but he did see Bitt praying often and reading his Bible for hours each day. One night, he spoke to Bitt and asked him, "You really believe in that book, don't you?"

Bitt replied, "I believe in it as much or more than you believe in yours." He was referring to Lala's Koran. He further told Lala, "I'm praying for you every night because I think you're a solid man. I just think you're on the wrong team."

That night, Lala woke Bitt up by pushing on the side of his bunk bed. Addressing Bitt as Pops, he asked him if they could talk. Bitt agreed to speak with him and got out of bed. Lala looked Bitt in the eye and said, "Tell me about Jesus Christ."

Bitt told him that Jesus was the only way to heaven and rose from the dead. He also informed him that there were not 144 virgins waiting in heaven for those who strapped on suicide vests and slaughtered innocent people. He explained, "Jesus came to this earth because my God and your Allah are so tough. If you're impressed with the radical ideology of your religion, you should know that the Lord God was the original gangster. He used to kill thousands at a time with his sword-wielding angels. He'd lead people into battle on the short side of hundred-to-one odds, and they'd fight for days at a time and wipe out their enemies. My opinion is that God got lonely and sent Jesus Christ to earth to save us all because there weren't too many people making it to heaven to spend eternity with him. It was him and a bunch of angels because nobody was worthy enough to make it. Jesus was a man who led a perfect life and allowed himself to be crucified so we could be forgiven of our sins. He did this for his people and for those who weren't even born yet. He took a terrible beating with straps embedded with glass and sharp objects made to rip the hide off of people. And he voluntarily took that for all of us. You can be proud to be a Christian, because in what other religion does someone rise from the dead like Jesus did? He came back from the grave. The other religious leaders, like Buddha, are dead as a doornail, but not Jesus. He brought men back to life. He gave sight to the blind and healed the lame."

When Bitt finished speaking, Lala just shook his head and said, "Okay," and that was it. The exchange was over, and Bitt didn't know if anything had sunk in with Lala or not. They went to their respective bunks and went to sleep. The next morning, the guards were yelling out to check who wanted to go outside to the tiny yard. As always, Bitt called out that he wanted to go. He looked at Lala and asked him if he wanted to go with him. Lala responded, "In the snow?"

Bitt replied, "Yeah." To his surprise, Lala said he too wanted to go outside. For the next two weeks, Lala accompanied Bitt to the outdoor area to exercise. They ran and worked out at a ferocious pace. They chased each other and did jumping jacks and push-ups. Lala convinced Bitt to do a lot of squats, which he added to his routine. At about that time, Lala quit speaking in their cell. Bitt wondered what was going on, and he started sleeping with one eye open, as he didn't know the state of Lala's mind.

The book cart came by one day, and both of them grabbed several. Bitt had enough time that he could exercise, read his Bible, and still read a fictional novel in a day or two. One night, Lala was looking at a book, and he began chanting in Arabic. It made Bitt a little nervous, and he prayed about it. He told God he knew God was in his corner, and he prayed for Lala to have an awakening. He went to sleep with the peace of a child. A few nights later, Lala woke Bitt up in the middle of the night and told him he had been reading the Bible. He asked Bitt if he thought everything in it was true. Bitt replied, "Yes, it's true, and I think you know it in your heart."

A few days later, Lala was allowed to make his monthly call. The frequency of phone usage was restricted to once every thirty days for prisoners in the hole. It could be a disappointing experience, because if no one answered or a line was busy, your next chance to call was thirty days away. Bitt always wrote to his family to let them know about when he planned to call. Lala made a call to his mother while Bitt waited to use the sole phone. Lala mostly listened and made only a few comments in his native language. Lala finished and had nothing to say to Bitt at that time.

However, in the middle of the night, Lala woke up Bitt again. He told him, "There's something to this Jesus Christ. He's for real."

Bitt was excited for him and responded, "Yeah, I've been telling you that, man."

Lala then asked Bitt if he could tell him something and proceeded to relay the following: "My mother is a devout Muslim woman, and my family is Muslim. I didn't come to prison and become a Muslim to get protection; I am a Muslim. My mother was going to a mosque last Sunday and was walking by a Christian church. Something made her go inside. I hadn't spoken to my mother for about ten months until the other day, even when I was in the compound and could have called her every day. Something made me go to that phone and call my mother the other day. My mother told me she was inside the church for ten minutes or so and was getting nervous. The next thing she knew, the sermon and the singing stopped. The preacher called out her name in the sanctuary. Then he called out my name, and he said directly to my mother, 'Don't worry about your son; he'll return to you a fine young man,' and he resumed the services."

Bitt listened to Lala, and the story scared him a little, as his world was suddenly rocked. As Bitt said, "I knew then that Christ was in my life and that I had done something worthy of him. For the first time, I felt that I had exemplified Jesus and done something Christlike. I felt like I was doing the right thing for the first time in my life in the worst of environments. At that moment, I knew that I had truly given myself to Jesus, and I was overcome with emotion." Bitt knew he had experienced a watershed moment, and his life would never be the same. His faith started growing in his heart from that point forward, and his love for God grew exponentially. He thought about how God had given him all kinds of signs over the years that he loved him, but Bitt had paid little or no attention to them and continued on his worldly path. He recalled that God had wrapped him in a cloth earlier in his imprisonment, and Bitt had still questioned him. But now, in the form of Lala, Bitt had touched somebody for the glory of Christ, and it was overwhelming. He knew that Jesus had guided him in forming his words to Lala. He reflected on the experience: "He had touched me and was in me. I had finally made room for God, and I felt the presence of the Holy Spirit in me. I had the devil in me for so long; it was incredibly powerful. He sent me one of the toughest guys in prison—and a Muslim to boot. It made me one of the happiest human beings in the world."

Lala was transferred out a few weeks later, but he and Bitt remained in touch by correspondence. Before he left, Lala was totally consumed with reading the Bible. He had many questions for Bitt, who prayed over many of them to be sure his answers were God-inspired. Bitt knew that Jesus Christ was speaking through him. Before he transferred to another facility, Lala prayed for Jesus to come into his heart and make him one of his followers. Bitt sent him away with his radio so he could listen to Christian programming. Lala was a new man but no more so than was Bitt. Bitt knew beyond a shadow of a doubt he was done with the girlie business and all that it entailed. He never went back to it.

CHAPTER 30

Bitt now knew he had wasted a lot of time when he could've been in a closer relationship with Jesus. He was determined to make the most of what time he had left in his life. He continued to work out daily in his cell and in the twenty-by-twenty-foot outdoor compound for the hole residents. He could tell the joints in his body were getting looser from his diligent exercise. With Lala transferred to another prison, Bitt was again by himself, which was fine by him. He spent his time praying and reading the Bible all day long. He also read his mail and answered letters consistently. He was on his best behavior with the guards other than making them take him outside. The hole's lieutenant of the guards asked Bitt to room with an inmate who was threatening suicide. He figured Bitt would at least inform the guards if the man tried to hang himself. Bitt agreed to take in the new roomie, and he used the opportunity to try to convince him of the importance of knowing Jesus. The transferred prisoner had no interest in talking and instead went on a starvation strike. Prison officials soon put him in a medical facility, and Bitt was again by himself. He switched cells and, luckily, got one with a shower that would pour water for five seconds before requiring the user to push a button over and over.

Bitt had made the transfer from a life in which he had it all, from the perspective of many. He'd previously enjoyed many worldly things at his disposal, including money, drugs, alcohol, women, celebrity friends, free tickets to major sporting events, multiple houses, power, swagger, trips to Vegas and other hot spots, and much more. He was the man wherever he went. He now knew that finding Jesus Christ's love and a feeling of peace and serenity was infinitely better than the pleasures that had been at his disposal in the past. He knew he had experienced a true spiritual awakening. Bitt came to realize that he hadn't known what constituted true love until he fully accepted Christ. He understood that he didn't have to make enough money to pave his street with gold, because he was now in a position to someday go to heaven, where the streets were paved with gold. He soon learned that everything that was to come his way was a blessing from God in some fashion.

Bitt continued to flourish in the hole, whereas most of his fellow inmates suffered to the point where they became mentally or physically unstable. After having a half dozen teeth pulled to relieve significant pain, he continued to work out and drop more weight. He ended up going down to 250 pounds and was all muscle. The lieutenant soon asked Bitt to take in another needy inmate. This one was a young, soft kid who was in danger of being molested in the general population. Bitt was promised extra food, extra clothes, and all of the time outside he wanted. He agreed to take in the youngster, and the guards were confident he wouldn't hurt him. During that time, Bitt was given added time to his sentence for the fight prior to going to the hole. He ended up spending an extra fifty-four days in prison before being eventually released. This added time was handed down by the prison court. Bitt couldn't go back to the general population, as the Hispanic inmates let it be known that they would kill him if they could get to him.

Bitt's new cellmate, in his early twenties, was small and soft and answered to Billy. He was meek and wore glasses. He grew to like Bitt, and he soon became comfortable living in the same cell with him. Bitt felt sorry for him because he knew he was going to have a hard time completing his sentence. They made a deal regarding their meals. Bitt gave him his cake in return for the youngster's vegetables. Bitt also got to eat his roommate's chicken, which was frequently served in different forms, and gave his new friend his desserts and his hamburgers, which looked more like sausages. Bitt also bought Billy Snickers and Reese's Peanut Butter Cups from the prison store. He tried to get the kid to exercise with him to no avail.

Bitt continued to work out and study the Bible. The cell rotation continued every thirty days, and he lucked out and got another cell with a shower. His cellmate stuck by him like glue and stayed in his cell with him for about three months until Bitt was moved to another prison. Bitt tried to minister to young Billy but saw no signs of his words having any effect on him. Billy gave Bitt no indication that he was moved by his message, but he did listen to everything he was told with at least mild interest. Since Bitt couldn't reenter the general population at Loretto, he was transferred temporarily to Canaan Federal Prison, about twenty miles east of Scranton, Pennsylvania. He was in their holding section for two weeks. Canaan had two-man cells but no weight room. He was back in general population, and he was allowed to go outside to a recreation area for several hours a day. Bitt kept his eyes down and his headset on while spending most of his time riding a stationary bicycle during his brief Canaan stint.

He was then sent to the Allenwood Federal Correction Complex in the spring of 2012. The authorities put Bitt in a cell with Lenny from Philadelphia. A Catholic man, Lenny was quickly respected by Bitt. He was a jailhouse lawyer who performed all of his own legal work and some for his fellow inmates. He was in his late fifties and a former wrestler for a Big Twelve school. He stood five foot nine and was heavily muscled from frequent workouts. He weighed about 175 pounds, down from 240 when he was initially incarcerated years earlier. He was serving a thirty-year term and was rumored to have ties with organized crime. He had a multifaceted portfolio and owned many businesses and properties that were run by his associates while he was jailed. He and Bitt became fast friends. Bitt came to learn that he had been released from prison several times but rearrested and convicted each time. He was a devout Catholic and was well thought of by the prison staff and his fellow inmates.

In his best shape for at least ten years, Bitt went out to the softball field and asked one of the A-team managers if he could play. The manager replied that his team was full, and he couldn't use Bitt. Then Bitt saw a Jamaican inmate from Loretto who knew he played at a high level. He invited Bitt to play for his team, and Bitt accepted. For the prisoners, playing in the A league was a big deal. Many inmates and guards watched the games, and the league afforded the participants some status and a chance to display their athletic talents. When the teams warmed up, Bitt declined the chance to join in, which surprised his teammates. The Jamaican Loretto transfer informed his manager that Bitt should pitch, and Bitt started on the mound, where he was gifted and comfortable. The opponents were the team managed by the inmate who'd turned Bitt down a short time earlier. One of the opposing players was a fleet-footed outfielder named Matt. Bitt and Matt would soon form a friendship. Matt later told Bitt that he knew he could play after Bitt threw the first pitch of the game, backed up fifteen feet to take a defensive position, and then deftly fielded a hot shot and threw out the runner with a hard throw to first. Matt turned to his manager and told him he was a fool for letting Bitt slip through his fingers.

Matt and Bitt began practice hitting on a daily basis for a couple of hours. They would pitch to each other to hone their skills. The guards hated these sessions because Matt, who had prodigious power, could hit balls over the prison field wall. Each time this occurred, a loud buzzer went off, and it required the guards to reset the security system. Bitt ramped up his workout routine and soon was down to 230 pounds of solid muscle. Matt was enthralled with Bitt's stories of past softball exploits and players with whom he had played on various teams. Somewhat skeptical of Bitt's stories, he asked his father to do some Internet research to back up the claims. It all checked out, and Matt developed a new level of respect for Bitt. There were a few times when Bitt talked to Matt about his faith, but his words had no effect as far as he could determine. Matt was released a couple of months later and went home to Michigan. He was a former engineer who had been arrested for selling crystal meth on the side.

With God in his heart, Bitt was on his best behavior at Allenwood. He didn't get into any fights, arguments, or side deals. He attended a white church briefly but was more impressed and inspired in the services conducted by the Hispanic inmates. He was given a reserved chair in the highly coveted twenty-four-chair

TV-viewing room. One of the inmates, an Asian from New York called Big Henry, was assigned with Bitt to mop floors in the area. Henry was five foot six and 285 pounds of muscle. A friendly guard allowed Bitt and Henry to watch television in the evenings when they were supposed to be working. They watched TV together for six weeks before Henry finally spoke to him. Lenny, the Catholic from Philadelphia, eventually vouched for Bitt, and Henry accepted him as a friend. Henry could lift more than 550 pounds on an incline, an impressive showing of strength. Bitt and Henry worked out together after Matt finished his sentence. Another inmate at Allenwood, Joe the Baker, also grew close to Bitt.

Chairs in the coveted TV room, arranged in six rows of four, were hard to come by. After a short time, Bitt was elevated to chair number three in the first row, after only Henry and Lenny. Guests could use an empty chair only with the permission of the owner. Henry effectively owned the TV room, and talking was not allowed. The guards didn't enter the room, as they respected Henry's physical stature and recognized his domain. A seat was given to the Baker at Bitt's request. The programming was dictated strictly by Henry, and some offerings on the agenda were *24,*

Breaking Bad, and *Sons of Anarchy*. Those not lucky enough to have assigned seats would line up outside the window to the room to see as much as possible since no TVs were allowed in the cells.

The Baker worked in the kitchen, and he had access to all types of food. He cooked fabulous meals for Bitt's cell and others. Bitt cut vegetables for the Baker, who was Canadian.

The Baker was eventually transferred to another federal institution in Pennsylvania and is still serving his sentence. Lenny, still in Allenwood, has been diagnosed with cancer.

CHAPTER 31

Surprisingly, drugs or alcohol never took over Bitt's life. He'd occasionally partied heavily, especially at Platinum 21, but he was too interested in making money to let that goal be affected by anything. His prison stint and accompanying spiritual growth allowed him to give up drugs and alcohol once and for all. He attended church and played softball at Allenwood, mostly with Hispanic prison mates, and kept his nose clean. His health improved, and his ability to run returned when he purposely lost some muscle mass in favor of achieving overall fitness. He was on top of the world despite the fact that he was incarcerated.

He began to believe he had a good chance to make something of his life when he was released. He was spiritually tuned in and considered himself to be a changed human being. He was looking forward to being reunited with his family. He didn't have another fight in prison. He did, however, have a bout with kidney stones. He prayed his way through the pain and finally passed them. It was another sign to him that his faith was his true salvation, both physically and emotionally. It was his second experience with stones, as he'd been treated in a Florida hospital several years earlier.

The Allenwood inmates formed more than a hundred groups of weight-lifting teams, known as cars. Bitt was bench-pressing 365 pounds and had his eye on hitting 400 or 405, when the big sickness suddenly occurred. A flu-like epidemic spread throughout the prison, and many of the inmates suffered from nausea, projectile vomiting, and explosive diarrhea. Then a curious thing happened: some of the prisoners began to disappear with no explanation.

For several weeks, no one was allowed out of his cell block. Some prisoners began passing out, and the guards were soon replaced by men wearing hazardous-material suits. Twenty or so inmates in Bitt's area were hauled off and never returned to their cells. No explanation was offered to Bitt or any of his fellow prisoners. It was unsettling for the jailed population, and everyone feared that he would begin having the flu-like symptoms. One old-timer voiced his opinion that the prisoners were some kind of guinea pigs for secret experiments, but no one truly knew what was going on.

The bug lasted for about ten days, and then the guards eventually returned to replace the hazmat-suited individuals. Bitt began to feel ill about a week after the isolation period started. He passed out and fell after taking a shower. However, he came to and, fortunately, didn't throw up or demonstrate any intestinal issues. The medical staff, perhaps being less than honest, told him that his symptoms might be due to diabetes. He thought it was some kind of outbreak. It took a month before he felt better, and the inmate lockdown lasted a total of three weeks. The guards all offered the same explanation: a so-called virus from a third-world prisoner was responsible for the temporary round of illnesses. As many as a hundred prisoners were removed when they became sick, and they never returned to the prison. Bitt and his crew never found out what happened to them.

The white Christian group in prison was considered weak by the Muslims and other faith groups, primarily because it was considered a haven for pedophiles and others just wanting protection from the general population. Therefore, the truth of Jesus Christ was sometimes downplayed because believers didn't want to be associated with weak prisoners. The white Christians in particular tended not to lift weights or play softball. Bitt read his Bible two to three hours a day and prayed for another hour. He didn't belong to a Bible study group but used the TV room for his reading and prayer time. His sole job responsibility at that institution was to empty the trash bins on the athletic fields. He didn't have a paying job at Allenwood, but his sisters sent money to his prison account for candy, toiletries, writing materials, mayonnaise, tuna, bread, batteries, and stamps. Bitt made an effort to stay in his lane and not make waves at Allenwood. He turned down several offers to make money in venues such as card games and cigarette trading. He did "borrow" some food from the kitchen occasionally to sell or to make meals for himself and his friends.

Following the additional days added to Bitt's sentence for fighting at Loretto, he was released to a halfway house in Atlanta on November 14, 2012. His time in that facility was to last for up to six months, although he was eligible to go home after working for ten weeks. There were about two hundred people in the facility. He hated it because it was painful being at home for a few hours and then returning to the halfway house. He considered hitting someone so he would be sent back to prison for six more months, which would allow him to avoid the halfway house entirely. He didn't follow through on that idea because he had no guarantee of being sent back to Allenwood over another federal prison, and six months of solitary confinement was possible. He was torn because total separation from his family was strangely easier than brief visits or occasional half-day respites at home followed by a return to the halfway facility.

Bitt decided to test himself through his choice of a postrelease job. He took a parking attendant job near a club close to the location of the former Platinum 21 he had managed for years. He wanted to prove he could refrain from going into a club, despite numerous invitations from the owner himself and former Platinum patrons who noticed him working across the street. Club employees who used to work for Bitt constantly asked him to come in, have a drink, and visit. They also sent dancers to try to lure Bitt into the club. He and a coworker parked cars for two local restaurants, and he never felt the urge to go into the strip joint. This gave him a small sense of accomplishment.

Bitt lost his parking attendant job because the Onyx, now rebuilt after Bitt's crew burned it, was just down the block. One

Jim Henninger

Sunday afternoon, Jack Galardi, still the owner of the Onyx, saw Bitt parking cars and reported his presence near his club. Bitt was working in his tenth week, and a federal officer pulled him off of the parking attendant job. He was questioned about his intent, and he replied that all of his contacts for employment opportunities were in that area. He was threatened with an additional three months in the halfway house, but after further consideration, he was allowed to go home.

He was fitted with an electronic ankle bracelet and told not to stray more than ninety yards from a government-issued PC installed in his home to monitor his whereabouts. At last, Bitt was back home. His home confinement lasted only three months, and he didn't break the rigid rules of the agreement. He worked out regularly and was eligible for passes to attend church and go to medical appointments. He called a specific phone number for the bracelet to be temporarily turned off so he could leave for a little while to approved destinations. He had to call the number again when he returned home to reinstate the monitoring process.

Bitt had some adjustment issues after returning home, as he went from living in a little box to a four-thousand-square-foot two-story home in Cumming. He found it difficult to put up with messes made by his kids, unmade beds, and clothing strewn on the floor. He experienced some anxiety over these issues and made the lives of his daughters and son slightly miserable by nagging them to be neater. He had yet to realize that neatness in a six-by-ten-foot cell was more significant than in a large home. He reinstated his disciplinarian father role, and slowly, things began to transition smoothly. Bitt's daughters thought he was too thin when he came home, and he began working out in a health club for three hours a day after dropping off his girls at school. Shortly after being released, he punched and knocked out an acquaintance at a local Publix grocery store when Bitt felt the man had disrespected one of his daughters, briefly touching her upper chest area. He feared this act of aggression might land him back in prison, but the culprit didn't press charges. The in-store video cameras caught the action, and the event was quickly shared by employees of the local Publix stores. Bitt even became friends with the guy, who happened to live in the same neighborhood.

CHAPTER 32

Bitt had no desire to continue working as a parking lot attendant, nor did he want to return to his former life in nightclub management. Some friends contacted him and offered him a salary of $2,000 per week to organize and operate their entertainment clubs. He quickly turned down the opportunity. It wasn't a possibility he could legally consider, even if he wanted to get back into that field. He was forbidden, as part of his formal release arrangement, to work in any nightclubs or restaurants that served alcohol. He also couldn't work in the security field or provide consulting services for security purposes for nightclubs. He couldn't work in the limousine business or in any capacity in the adult entertainment field. He also was barred from working in the professional fight business in the form of managing fighters or promoting matches. He was not allowed to work in any form as a subcontractor for the federal or state government. He was effectively unable to use any of the skill set he'd developed over the years, but that didn't deter his determination to once again succeed economically. At the age of fifty-five, he was faced with the task of reinventing himself, but he felt he was up to the challenge.

He received other offers, including one to become involved in the sale of pain medication with a crooked physician. Another was proffered in the form of teaming up with a former acquaintance to rob drug dealers, something Bitt had excelled at doing in the past. He gave none of these options serious consideration, even though all of them offered easy, big money. However, Bitt's world was about to be rocked to his core. On December 9, 2012, less than a month after having his ankle bracelet removed, he was told he had cancer and was going to die. Nothing was ever the same after that soul-shaking news.

Occasional abdominal pain was a regular event for him in prison. Bitt would have intense cramps for several hours, which kept him bedfast. He would lie still and pray until the debilitating discomfort passed. This time, a few weeks after his release, the pain was unrelenting, prompting him to seek medical care. Bitt canceled a planned trip to Texas to visit a mattress factory. He had cultivated an interest in that industry after meeting a fellow prisoner who had made a successful living selling mattresses and furniture. Two friends from his nightclub days had agreed to front him $100,000 to get started. The investors were going to loan Bitt start-up cash with the expectation of being repaid at 50 percent interest. Bitt planned to pay himself $1,000 a week initially. He had already located a storefront in Cumming and had gone so far as to arrange a prospective leasing arrangement for his backers to sign. He was optimistic after spending a few days shadowing a mattress store owner and operator in Atlanta, an experience set up by his incarcerated buddy at Allenwood.

Still displaying an impressive level of business acumen, Bitt had already planned to use the $100,000 seed money to pay a few months of the lease and hold a grand opening with hot dogs and Cokes for prospective customers. He had identified a mattress manufacturer and was going to buy an initial stock of two hundred mattresses. He planned to advertise in the local paper and mail out flyers. He was going to spend about $40,000 on opening expenses, including the two hundred mattresses, and keep the remaining $60,000 on hand as an operating cushion. He was planning to be a one-man operation. Unfortunately, he became sick on a Sunday night, and the aggressive treatment regimen put a quick stop to his plans to open a business.

Bitt was informed that he had stage IV liver and colon cancer. He asked if he could go home from the hospital. The physician laughed and told him he'd be in the hospital for a while. A colonoscopy revealed a massive cancerous blockage in his intestines that was preventing him from having a bowel movement. It was confirmed that his colon cancer was in the final stages. The surgeon guaranteed he would not die during surgery. At precisely the correct moment, his friend Larry Townsend came to visit him. As one of the initial First Baptist Church of Cumming members to speak with Bitt when he began attending church years earlier, Townsend was the perfect godly man for the situation. Bitt told Townsend he was concerned about his twin daughters and what would become of them if he died. He knew his family would be willing to take them, but his mother and sisters were of an age that raising two preteen girls wouldn't necessarily be the best situation. Townsend suggested they pray over the matter. Bitt asked the Lord to give him the wisdom and courage to make arrangements for the best way to take care of his daughters. Over time, God would give Bitt an answer as to whom God wanted the girls to live with after he was gone.

Following his colon surgery, Bitt woke up to find his immediate family and Townsend at his side. He asked Townsend to come a little closer, and Bitt whispered to him, "Larry, I know who God wants to take the girls when I'm gone. He wants them to be with the youth minister's family or the family of one of their friends." Bitt knew the youth minister well from many discussions with him and the pastor about his salvation. He had only met the other man, who owned a company that appraised distressed properties, a couple of times, as the twins played youth sports with his daughter. However, he trusted his Maker and was certain that one of these two families was the right choice to raise his girls. He felt at peace with the decision and told this to Townsend. Both of the families knew about Bitt's background but were undeterred.

Between December 9 and December 23, 2012, Bitt had three more surgical procedures. He was released to go home for Christmas. After recuperating for a couple of weeks following the holidays, he started chemotherapy sessions in early January 2013. He was on an emotional roller coaster, and all thoughts of opening a business were dashed. He expected to live no more than sixty to ninety days. The members of First Baptist heard of Bitt's dilemma, and an amazing thing happened: no fewer than six families, after learning of Bitt's health problems, eventually stepped forward and offered to adopt Bitt's daughters after his demise. He was overcome with emotion, gratitude, and spiritual peace. Nothing in his colorful life had as powerful an effect on him as the love and willingness to sacrifice shown to him by these God-fearing brothers and sisters in Christ. Bitt felt like a lucky man despite his dire health outlook.

CHAPTER 33

Although he expected to die, he went to chemotherapy sessions as scheduled. He also spent at least two hours a day reading the Word. Bitt proved to himself that he was a Christian when he worked as a parking lot attendant across the street from his old nightclub. He felt a sense of pride that he didn't relent to pressure from acquaintances to go back to the club life or even just go for a visit. He felt strong for not giving in to the temptations of his former life. As a result, he felt grounded, clearheaded, spiritually healthy, and pure of heart. He gave up being the man and having lots of money, power, unlimited female companionship, influence, and other perks. He was convinced he had passed a big test, as he was out of prison and hadn't set foot in a club. He felt stronger and more courageous every day and knew he was done with his former way of life.

After coming home big, strong, and lean, Bitt was suddenly stricken with weakness and a death sentence courtesy of cancer. His plan to open a mattress store and support his family was gone. He had envisioned himself expanding into the furniture business down the road. He underwent two surgeries involving his colon, one on his liver, one on the colon, and a fifth procedure to place a port in his neck area to receive the chemotherapy concoctions. Bitt was living on a family pooling of resources, mostly funded by one of his sisters, who helped pay the bills for him and his kids. The generosity of his family kept things afloat during his next several months of treatment. He endured sixty-hour weekly sessions of chemotherapy delivered through a bag he wore over the next eighteen months. His sessions were on Mondays through Wednesdays. His physicians, including his primary oncologist, were shocked that he was holding up so well to the treatment.

Bitt's reaction to the chemotherapy was a blessing. He felt the normal nausea and temporary weakness but still had the energy to drive his daughters to school and take care of his yard. The treatments affected his sleeping pattern, and he found he was unable to fall asleep one night a week. But he did well, and after six months of treatment, he felt good enough to work out with weights. Another sign that Bitt was handling the treatments well was that he gained twenty pounds while receiving chemotherapy. By all appearances, he looked normal during the year and a half of treatment from 2013 to 2014. His sisters, who had taken care of Bitt's children during his prison stay, went home and allowed Bitt to manage his household.

Bitt's children all did well during that time, despite the fact that the twin sisters had to deal with the death of their mother, Rhonda Woodard, from cancer in late 2012, just before Bitt's release from prison. Bella, Bitt's oldest daughter, blossomed into a wonderful mother with two precious children. His son gave up on his promising baseball career despite the fact he was already drawing interest from Georgia Tech by his freshman year of high school. He is currently a professional poker player and finished in the top hundred in the national poker rankings in 2015. A catcher, he quit playing at age fifteen, and Bitt had mixed feelings about his occupational choice in that he felt some responsibility for it. He'd indirectly introduced his son to card games when he was growing up by hiring babysitters who were also club employees. They taught the youngster different card games, and he won $75,000 in an online tournament at age fourteen, playing under

Bitt's name. The boy gave up baseball when Bitt went to prison, and he became the man of the house. He later told Bitt that he felt as if he had lost his coach when his dad was incarcerated. Bitt was proud of his boy, who continued to utilize Bitt's home as a base for his card-playing activities. He began traveling to Las Vegas and other venues for weeks at a time to play in tournaments and related events.

Bitt utilized his ties with his brothers and sisters in Christ at First Baptist Church of Cumming to stay persistent in witnessing to others and reading the Gospel. His desire to tell others about Jesus Christ was his primary focus instead of feeling sorry for himself or worrying about his health. He continued to look for jobs at grocery stores and other retail outlets. His ex-convict status prevented him from being hired anywhere. He was not able to be bonded, which prevented him from being hired to work in an Atlanta-area appraisal business that inspected homes in danger of being foreclosed.

The chemotherapy seemed to be working at first, but in 2014, doctors told Bitt he was slipping. The cancer had gotten the upper hand and was again spreading, particularly in his colon and liver. Once again, his prospects for survival seemed slim. He was referred to a specialist affiliated with Atlanta's St. Joseph's Hospital. This physician, an ex-military man, had served in a Special Forces unit in the Middle East. He and Bitt hit it off, as they both shared experiences they'd had overseas while serving their country. Of course, Bitt's service was mostly off the books for the CIA, which had helped him receive a reduced federal prison sentence.

The doctor told Bitt that he had a 30 percent chance of surviving only if he agreed to submit to a risky operation. He told Bitt that the biggest concern was if he developed an infection, which would reduce his survival chances to 10 to 20 percent. But without the surgery, he had no chance. The procedure was quickly scheduled and took place two days after the consultation. Bitt was hospitalized for a little more than a month, and he developed an infection that required his port to be removed. He was in intensive care, and the port removal occurred under a canopy in his room to prevent his infection from spreading. The removal of the port should have taken thirty to forty-five minutes, but his weight-lifting activities had embedded the device in his chest wall, requiring it to be dug out. Bitt was given a local but started to complain of chest pain after an hour of digging.

The nurses helping with the removal were surprised that Bitt was able to stand the pain. When they expressed their concern to the surgeon, he told them to not worry about Bitt, because he was a "tough old bird." Bitt was sent home after ten days in recovery but was in terrible shape and extremely weak. He required in-home nursing care, including IV administration and treatment for diabetes. After a month, he grew weaker and returned to the hospital for a month of intensive treatment, including more chemotherapy. He began feeling better soon after and recovered to the point that he felt he had experienced a miracle. He knew that God had once again allowed him to bounce back from adversity and poor health. He even began lifting weights again, this time with his First Baptist Church buddy, the youth minister.

About that time, Bitt became friendly with some young Mormons canvassing his neighborhood on their bicycles. They wore black pants, long-sleeved white shirts, and black ties. Bitt invited them into his house, and soon they began working out with him. Unshaken in his faith, Bitt ministered to the young men by telling them the truth but not condemning them for their beliefs. He was impressed with their devotion to their faith, and he respected their tenacity. Bitt tried to influence the young men with the truth of the scripture and give them reason to doubt the

Book of Mormon. Bitt's house became a regular stop for the ever-changing pairs of young Mormons canvassing the area, and Bitt welcomed each and every one of them, telling them about Jesus and the Word.

Bitt went so far as to attend services at a local Mormon church on two occasions. He decided to see firsthand what his acquaintances believed in. He even read a few pages of Joseph Smith's bible, but he continued to talk to his frequent visitors about Jesus and the truth. The visits to Bitt's house continued for over a year, and he eventually enlisted his youth minister friend to come over to help him testify to the youngsters. Bitt felt led by the Lord to speak to the Mormons and put a seed or thought in their heads about the gospel of Jesus. He was careful to express his doubts about the Joseph Smith story and his so-called experiences without appearing heavy-handed. The visits abruptly stopped in late 2015 for no obvious reason. He never learned exactly why the young men stopped appearing at his doorstep, although he didn't feel much of a connection with the last two who visited him.

CHAPTER 34

In 2015, Bitt joined a new local health club, Atlanta Fitness of Cumming. He was feeling good and exercising hard. He worked out a few times with the visiting Mormon youngsters at the club before their visits stopped. He worked with a new pair every few months and often received greetings from former visitors who recalled their times with him fondly. Bitt missed his mentoring relationship with the Mormons.

His chemotherapy treatments started up again four months after his 2014 procedure at St. Joseph's and continued through the end of 2015. In late 2014, Bitt took part in strenuous weight-lifting sessions during which he performed a pyramid, a session in which the lifter engages in diminishing numbers of repetitions at a challenging weight. Bitt was working out with a friend of his son's and took him up and down a pyramid, an exhausting task. Continuing his workout, he was flat-benching 305 pounds, impressing his fellow weight lifters. They couldn't believe he was lifting so diligently while in cancer treatment. He always told the others in the club that he gave all of the credit for his strength to Jesus Christ. Not long afterward, he was lifting in his basement, and something in his upper body popped. He suddenly was able to lift only 50 percent of his previous weight, and he never regained his vitality. At a medical appointment a short time later, his oncologist told him he may have had a mild stroke or a heart attack. He also expressed his concern over the fact that Bitt was trying to lift such significant amounts.

Bitt made one more attempt to find a job, this one at the local Publix, where he had previously knocked out his neighbor. He was popular with the store employees and shopped there on a regular basis. He was on a first-name basis with most of them. The store manager wanted to hire him but told him his hands were tied. He explained that he knew Bitt would be a great employee and store representative to the customers, but his convicted-felon status prevented the manager from bringing him on board. Every opportunity to work was unsuccessful due to his convicted-felon status. He began caring for his twin girls and learned a new respect for women who stayed home to raise their children and run a home.

He knew his worth in the nightclub industry was intact, and he was a much-desired manager and security person. Offers continued to come in, and he refused them all. He managed to get by financially via the grace of God. He experienced countless episodes of discounts and other blessings for him and his family. His remaining residence in the Wynfield neighborhood was owned by one of his sisters to prevent any possibility of the government seeking ownership of it. The sister coordinated paying the bills, a return of sorts considering Bitt's repeated episodes of generosity to his family in the past. There were some setbacks, as some of the parents of schoolmates of Kalie and Calie refused to allow their children to associate with Bitt's girls when they learned of his background. However, most of the time, he found that others were supportive and even willing to become his friends and Christian supporters. The First Baptist staff, Larry Townsend, and other church members were there spiritually for Bitt and his twin girls. Bitt attributed all of this good fortune and love to his relationship with Christ.

Another pleasant surprise in his postprison life was longtime acquaintance Larry Reed. Bitt had hired Reed in the past as a bouncer, and their friendship stood the test of time. Bitt guided Reed through the Bible, although Reed was still in the industry, working at a seedy Atlanta club. Reed worked security and earned a six-figure salary, and Bitt, who counseled him to quit the nightclub industry, served as his mentor. He spoke frequently with Reed and occasionally sat with him in church services. Bitt had met him when he hired him as a bouncer in the early 2000s at the behest of an acquaintance who wanted distance from Reed, who had become hot with respect to the local law authorities. Reed was present on a particular night in the early 2000s when one of Bitt's former wives called him to come home because something was wrong with the family. Bitt rushed to her home with Reed in tow. Reed stayed outside, and a short time later, Bitt returned to the car with a head injury. He told Reed that his wife had been unruly, and he decided to leave after making sure nothing was awry. He asked Reed if he thought he should go to the hospital, and Reed told him it might be a good idea since he might need medical attention for his wound. While being treated, Bitt refused to give any details to the medical staff or the authorities, as he considered the matter to be personal and closed. He did promise a local police captain that he was not interested in any type of retribution, and there would be no dead bodies found in the morning for which he was responsible.

Bitt's twins immersed themselves in girls' grade-school basketball in Cumming and blossomed due to some godly coaches. They played recreational basketball for a First Baptist member and learned about more than just the sport. The twins came up with a personal goal to pursue: make sure every girl on the team scored at least one point during the season. That was a daunting task, as some of them had never registered a point in any form of organized play and couldn't reach the rim when trying to shoot. By the second game, all of the team members had scored. Bitt considered this desire by his daughters to be another God thing that he wouldn't have recognized as such in the past. The girls also participated in the annual Holiday Hoops basketball camp for local youth at Dobbs Creek Community Center in Cumming, further honing their skills while making new friends.

The talented twins were invited to participate in a girls' feeder basketball program in Cumming as their on-court skills blossomed. Bitt's job became seeking the best opportunities for the twins to stay active in basketball and develop their skills to the fullest extent possible. They eventually played up at their school, King's Ridge Christian School in Alpharetta, Georgia, and were allowed to compete with the girls' team one grade ahead of them. The support of the King's Ridge teachers and staff overwhelmed Bitt. Teachers and coaches attended the girls' summer basketball games and showed them unconditional love, as did parents of classmates of the twins. Further support and love for the twins came from their sixth-grade AAU basketball coach and his wife. Even the King's Ridge boys' high school basketball coach was a mentor to them. He organized and operated a youth basketball camp the girls attended, and he gave them special attention and guidance. More important than the apparent sports-related opportunities for Kalie and Calie at King's Ridge, they were cherished and nurtured in a loving and caring Christian educational environment.

A local family was instrumental in leading the twins to eventually enroll at King's Ridge, and they treated the girls as if they were their own children during periodic sleepover events in their home with their daughter. At every turn, God allowed Bitt to make Christian friends while guiding his twins in their basketball pursuits. He instilled a competitive spirit in the girls, tempered with a sense of fair play and respect for their opponents. He taught them to strive to win but to graciously accept losses with maturity and love for others when they occurred.

Bitt was repeatedly blessed to make great Christian friends after he promised God to stay out of the club industry after being released from prison. He discovered that friends demonstrated unconditional love and weren't just people you paid to do something for you. These great brothers and sisters in Christ included the youth minister's wife. She became the twins' substitute mother, and she and her husband agreed to adopt them whenever Bitt lost his battle with liver and colon cancer. This arrangement was formalized, and the guardianship of the girls was transferred from Bitt's sister. Bitt had a feeling of peace that the welfare of his twins would be settled after he joined his Savior in heaven. He was confident that the adopting parents would raise the girls and love them as if they were their own. They went so far as to offer to let Bitt move into their home when his illness required daily living assistance. He remained grateful for being truly forgiven of his sins. He'd thought he was completely lost and beyond redemption for his years of involvement in corruption, crime, and sin. He became comfortable with his life, including his poor health outlook. He knew his life was finally leading to heaven, and he saw

God's love daily from simple things, such as walking in his yard and talking with his neighbors. He knew that God loved him and counted every hair on his head.

He had recollections of numerous dangerous events with bullets and fists flying, and he came to understand that he'd been under the protection of God's hand, although he'd done nothing to deserve it. He thanked God every day for sending him to prison, thereby saving his life. He also thanked God every day for sending cancer to him in order to draw him closer to God. He harbored no anger toward his Maker but only gratitude for the time on earth he was granted. He lost his physical prowess but gained much more from a spiritual standpoint. He had peace regarding the welfare of his children and their outcomes. He was particularly proud of his son, a self-sufficient young man. He gave him credit for growing up and becoming a man early despite facing several of his teenage years without his dad around. The twins were set up for a Christian upbringing and godly lives. Bitt knew he was clearly on the path to everlasting life with the Lord Jesus. Blessed beyond measure by his Maker, he made the transition from crime to Christ, from nightlife to eternal life.

EPILOGUE

After a grueling four-year battle with cancer, Bitt went to be with the Lord on October 11, 2016, at the age of fifty-nine. He was faithful to the end, and even when dealing with excruciating pain, he spoke lovingly of his Savior, his family, and his many blessings. He left behind three daughters, including thirteen-year-old twins, and a twenty-three-year-old son. He was a positive influence on many people with whom he came into contact, and he spoke to Atlanta-area youth groups and Bible study groups during the last months of his life. The following three documents speak eloquently about his influence and how deeply he was loved. The first paragraphs were written by his daughters, Kalie and Calie. They were submitted to King's Ridge Christian School in Alpharetta to fulfill a requirement for consideration of enrollment. The girls were eleven years old at the time. Both works speak volumes of the influence of Bitt in their young lives. The final document is the obituary written and delivered during Bitt's funeral service by his devoted friend and mentor Larry Townsend of Cumming and First Baptist Church. It is a heartfelt tribute to Bitt and a fitting conclusion to this book.

Kalie thrower

God has given me many blessings, gifts, and talents. My goal in life is to do everything in love. 1 Corinthians 16:14 "Let everything you do be done in love." This verse inspires me and has shown me a gift that god has given me. He gave me a giving heart I've truly learned that it is better to give than receive. My family and I aren't wealthy in dollars, but we are wealthy in the love and faith we have in Jesus Christ our Lord and Savior. Here is a simple story that shows the gift God gave me and how it affected somebody else.

    Our team had entered a basketball tournament in Covington Ga it was located at Newton high school. After our team had just competed we all decided to watch and check out our next opponents for the next game. I couldn't help but notice a girl that was playing with a shoe almost the size of my dads I was apprehensive and told my dad, but as I kept pondering on the thought of how immense and ill-fitting the shoes were the more I felt guilty for how many times I didn't appreciate something that was given to me. I soon realized that the family was in truth poor. The girl had been wearing her older brother's shoes that they both shared as the third quarter starter we saw her having to take them off and give to her brother so he could compete in his game leaving her with a raggedy pair of tennis shoes. My family and I felt the lord spirit in our hearts pushing us to try and help this young lady. My father had gotten in touch with the coach and got all the information needed to help her. We went out and bought her a radiant red colored shoe to go with her team colors and a couple pairs of socks to match. My dad met up with the coach and gave him the gifts to give to her we wanted it to be anonymous because the bible preaches in Acts 20:35 "It is more blessed to give than to receive." I hope she feels that people care and that jesus is like the wind you don't see him but you feel him. God gave me a gift that my have changed a young lady's faith in jesus Christ.

Calie Thrower

God has gave me the gift to see life in a better perspective, by believing in him. God has blessed me to be in a family that is Christian based and teaches me the moral and Christian values. I don't and never will desrive any gifts from God. God has always been there for my family and I, even when we doubt our faith. God has also blessed me with good health and actions toward others.

God had also given me a very big talent. God has allowed me to have speed, strength, and anything you need to be an athlete. I plan to use those talents to glorify God. Those talents have allowed me to play on teams and meet wonderful families and friends that will always be there for me. God has given my family and I so much that we don't deserve, but he keeps on giving, that's what makes him God.

God has given my family and I good and caring hearts. Over the summer during on of our basketball tournament we helped a man spiritually and physically.

The first two days (from driving back from the gym) my dad recognized a man lying down on the bench. He first went by himself, brought him food and asked if there was anything he needed. The next day my sister and I met him and brought him some food, water, and Gatorade. We came back daily to help him. We asked the hotel fir extra supplies this man could use. They gave us blankets, covers, sheets, and pillows, along with the clothing and essentials we bought him. We ended up sharing our faith to him and I think he came to know Christ. Its crazy how God can work in peoples lives, even though that man had nothing, he could still find Christ. My family an I still think about him and pray for him. I feel great for helping Mr. Charels Edwards Mittchell, and I hope he still believes in Christ.

God is great and he does everything to help us closer to him and able for us to spread the News of Jesus Christ to people so they can go to heaven and spend eternal life with him. God has gave me amazing family and friends. God has blessed me so much with everything. God is truly amazing.

On a Sunday morning in 1996 I was seated with our First Baptist Church choir; thus, I could see the whole congregation. The service had started and were worshiping in song. It was then that I saw a big, big man walk in and take a seat near the rear of the church to my left. He was impeccably dressed in a suit that probably cost a thousand dollars or more, shirt and tie to match, and hair slicked back in a neat ponytail. I remember thinking, "What is that dude doing here?" The next thing I noticed was that he was singing every word of the hymns we were singing. It was at that point I realized that this wasn't close to his first time in a church, and I probably spent more time watching and wondering about him than paying attention to the sermon. Well, shame on me for that. I don't recall getting to speak to him after church; however, the next Sunday I saw him and made a point of meeting him and welcoming him to First Baptist. He introduced himself as Bitt Thrower, and I could see the irony in the name Bitt, for he was about six four, probably 275 pounds, and all man, but was as polite and respectful of our age difference as he could be.

I don't know why, but I was drawn to this man in a way that I didn't understand until much later in our relationship. As our friendship grew, I found myself counseling him as if he were a son, and I grew to love him as one. I learned of things in his life that reminded me of myself when I was totally consumed by the world and wanted absolutely nothing to do with God. I think it was reciprocal, for he once stated that he wanted to thank me for not letting up or giving up on him.

I saw him transformed from a man of the world back to one of the teaching and training he received from his parents as a youth. Every time I saw him, he unashamedly bear hugged me, kissed me on the cheek and said, "I love you Mister Larry or Brother." In deference to our age, he never ever allowed himself to call me Larry. Bitt was a man who, as we say, never forgot his raisin', his family, or his God. Be assured, I am convinced beyond a doubt, that our God never forgot him or gave up on him, and that today though his body lies here, his soul is at rest with his Savior for eternity.

CPSIA information can be obtained
at www.ICGtesting.com
Printed in the USA
FFOW03n0805020218
44816283-44984FF